Dining In—Philadelphia

COOKBOOK

A Collection of Gourmet Recipes for Complete Meals
from the Philadelphia Area's finest Restaurants

MARILYNN MARTER

FOREWORD BY ELAINE TAIT

Peanut Butter Publishing
Seattle, Washington

HDL Publishing
Costa Mesa, California

Publisher: Elliott Wolf
Editor: Phyllis Stein Novack
Coordinator: Bailey Alexander
Production: Melonie Branson
Illustration: Barbara Alexander

Copyright © 1988 by Peanut Butter Publishing
329 Second Avenue West, Seattle, Washington 98119
ISBN 0-89716-202-1

CONTENTS

TITLES IN SERIES

FOREWORD

Anyone who fantasizes that owning and running a restaurant would be fun is quickly relieved of that notion.

Anyone who dreams of writing a book on restaurants because he or she thinks it would be fun, hasn't talked to me or Marilynn. There's a hellish amount of detail-conscious work involved. In recent months, Marilynn, whom I've known and valued as a friend and food colleague for a dozen years, has been saying "no" to all but the most pressing social invitations because there was a restaurant to be visited, a recipe to be tested or a paragraph to be written for this book.

She cares very much that it be done properly. And that makes her the perfect person to write this chapter in the ongoing history of Philadelphia restaurants. Until the early 1970s, you didn't have a great choice of dining destinations in the City of Brotherly Love. But from the Bicentennial mid-'70s on, Philadelphia has moved steadily towards becoming America's restaurant city.

There were those who called what happened here a Restaurant Renaissance. That sounded catchy but it didn't accurately describe a city enamored with restaurant dining for the first time in its long, colorful history. Restaurants in the '70s were often the enterprises of dedicated amateurs. They were started with not much more than a few dollars for thrift shop furniture, some used kitchen equipment and a couple of Julia Child cookbooks. To stay in business was another story.

Rents got higher, competition stiffer. Many early restaurants didn't survive. But a surprising number are still here and I'm pleased to see that Marilynn has included a sampling of these oldies but goodies, including Sansom Street Oyster House and Victor Cafe among her selections for the book. She has given you a taste of the best of the newer places as well as palaces like DiLullo Centro and The Fountain at the Four Seasons Hotel, along with homey, fun spots like the White Dog Cafe and Pyrenees. Above all, her choices are representative of the many caring restaurants in our city. Philadelphians as well as those who envy us our treasure trove of good dining establishments will enjoy duplicating some of the dishes local kitchens do so well. There's something for everyone in these pages from very easy to quick and still stylish recipes to be made often to more complicated creations designed to star at special occasions.

—Elaine Tait

PREFACE

For someone who can spend half the dinner hour trying to decide which of two tempting dishes to order, narrowing the list of fine restaurants to 21 was as difficult as pinning some chefs to specific measurements. They are, after all, accustomed to adding a pinch here, a splash there until a dish tastes or looks just right.

In the end, that is how this book came together—a dash of different styles, a pinch of different neighborhoods until a good balance of flavors in recipes and techniques was reached. Each restaurant here sets a high and caring standard for food and service. Each qualifies as a personal favorite, a place where (as those in the business or on expense accounts are apt to say) I spend my own money.

The Philadelphia restaurant scene is an ever-changing one and the same players often take many parts. This almost familial network within our restaurant community is traced here, in part, in the histories of Alouette, Le Bec-Fin, Flying Fish and the 16th Street Bar & Grill, all of which share common roots. Similarly, DiLullo, Apropos and the White Dog Cafe each bear the stamp of the same talented chef.

I hope you will enjoy reading about these restaurants and the talented people who run them, and that you will find the recipes tempting enough to try in your own kitchen as I have in mine.

A few of the recipes here are longtime favorites that remain on the menu year round. Others are seasonal in nature. It is because restaurant menus change so often that some of the best dishes are preserved here in recipe form. Among them you will note ingredient trends like raspberry vinegar and eggplant.

Some recipes look long and complicated, too complicated to tackle perhaps. But, as in restaurant kitchens, a little organization goes a long way. The recipes are designed to show the system of assembling grand cuisine to order. The format of this book is such that the rule of reading a recipe through before beginning to cook is all the more essential. Some dishes are "composed" of separate preparations, many of which must or can be made in advance. In some cases, the recipe for one of these components may be found elsewhere in the book. Items shown in CAPITAL LETTERS will be found as sub-recipes following the main recipe. Items, other than proper names, beginning with a Capital Letter appear elsewhere and are listed in the Recipe Index.

For those still shy of stocks, today's home cook can shortcut even a master chef's recipe if he or she must. There is acceptable, ready-made Brown Sauce and Demi-Glace to be found in area supermarkets and specialty food shops. Other preparations also may be conveniently simplified by using ready-made versions of pasta, pastry, tartshells and such. If costly ingredients like lobster are out of your budget, consider substitutions like shrimp or monkfish. For convenience, equivalent measurements are given to aid in purchasing ingredients or to simplify the measuring. Techniques and times have been adapted, when possible, to home kitchens and equipment. Details and descriptions are included where they seemed relevant, but the recipes do assume some basic knowledge of cooking terms and techniques, and some degree of personal judgement and taste. After all, that's what makes cooking fun. Should you have questions about any of the recipes, you may write to: Marilynn Marter, Food Writer, P.O.Box 8263, Philadelphia, PA 19101. Meanwhile, welcome to the world of Philadelphia restaurants.

— Marilynn Marter

ACKNOWLEDGMENTS

My special thanks to Elaine Tait for her encouragement, to my family and friends for their patient support and to the chefs who so willingly shared their time and recipes.

Dinner for Four

Sliced Salmon with Tomato and Ginger Cream

Mixed Greens with Raspberry Vinaigrette

Filet Mignon with Gorgonzola Cheese Sauce

Poached Pear Anglaise

Wines:

With the Salmon—Rutherford Hill Chardonnay
With the Salad—Burgess Zinfandel, 1982
With the Filet—Stag's Leap Cabernet Sauvignon, 1983
With the Pear—Schramsberg Cremant, 1983

Michel Wakim, Proprietor/Chef
George Wakim and Joseph Wakim, Managers

L ebanon-born Michel Wakim was still in his teens when he came to America in the early '70s to study engineering. While following the course familiar to so many students and aliens— get a restaurant job, work nights, get a free meal, meet people—he found his future.

But that came a bit later. In between, he brought his two brothers and mother to America. His mother taught him to cook Lebanese dishes. The brothers got restaurant jobs.

"Coming from a Third World Country, women there have time to prepare feasts for their families. That gave me a good palate as a child. My mother always bought the best," he recalls.

Wakim's educated palate proved an advantage. Soon he was studying the best French and American cookbooks and experimenting in the kitchen. Gradually his goals changed. He gave up engineering, ruled out the possibility of returning to his war torn homeland and decided to go into the restaurant business. Mostly he was determined to be a success.

"I always wanted to have my own business," he says. "I was brought up with the attitude of not working for anyone."

In 1980 he opened Allegresse, its name the Latin word for joy and happiness. The Main Line restaurant has an overall Gallic feel. Patrons dine in an intimate atmosphere reminiscent of a French home dining room. By 1983, the business had blossomed to include another restaurant, Evviva, a mile or so down the road in Narberth. Wakim also does some catering and is consultant to Allegro, a food distributor.

"I like to keep food simple and let it taste the way it should," says Wakim. "And I like to concentrate on daily specials, rather than doing the same thing over and over. I don't like to do what everyone else is doing."

281 Montgomery Avenue
Bala Cynwyd

SLICED SALMON WITH TOMATO AND GINGER CREAM

1 *pound fillet of salmon*	1 *teaspoon oil*
1 *egg, beaten*	*TOMATO AND GINGER*
	CREAM

1. Diagonally slice salmon into 8 medallions, about 2 ounces each. Dip slices in egg. In non-stick pan, heat oil and sauté 2 to 3 minutes until just barely opaque.
2. Pool TOMATO AND GINGER CREAM on warm plates and place 2 prepared salmon medallions on each. Garnish, if desired, with tomato rose and fans of blanched snowpeas.

Wakim doesn't like to cover food with sauce, he says, because it masks the dish. Salmon is the most popular fish at the restaurant, but don't hesitate to substitute other firm-fleshed species like swordfish, monkfish, tuna, even shark, in dishes like this.

TOMATO AND GINGER CREAM

1 *ounce ginger root, peeled,*	½ *cup heavy cream*
sliced very thin and minced	2 *tablespoons unsalted butter*
½ *cup tomato concasse (tomato*	
that has been peeled, seeded	
and diced)	

Combine ginger and tomato concasse in a non-aluminum saucepan. Bring to a boil and simmer 2 to 3 minutes. Add cream and stir until blended. Over low heat, whisk in butter just before serving.

MIXED GREENS WITH RASPBERRY VINAIGRETTE

2 oranges, peeled
1 head bibb lettuce
1 bunch arugula (4 ounces)
1 bunch watercress (4 ounces)

4 leaves Belgian endive,
  julienned
½ cup RASPBERRY
  VINAIGRETTE
¾ cup raspberries
½ cup enoki mushrooms

1. Cut oranges into sections, remove seeds and side membranes.
2. Combine greens (cut or tear as needed) and place in a bowl.
3. Toss with *RASPBERRY VINAIGRETTE*; divide on plates.
4. Top with orange sections, raspberries and mushrooms.

Thinly sliced medallions or strips of cooked duck or other poultry make a wonderful addition to this salad. Just arrange a fan of sliced meat on the greens.

RASPBERRY VINAIGRETTE

¼ cup best quality olive oil
¼ cup walnut oil
¼ cup raspberry vinegar
¼ cup raspberries, puréed
  and strained

2 teaspoons minced shallot,
  optional
½ teaspoon sugar
½ teaspoon salt
  Dash of white pepper

Combine all ingredients in blender and mix well. Makes about 1 cup.

FILET MIGNON WITH GORGONZOLA CHEESE SAUCE

2 pounds fillet of beef (have
  butcher cut 4 8-ounce slices
  or 8 4-ounce slices)
¼ pound (1 stick) unsalted
  butter

3 shallots, minced
1½ cups ruby port
6 tablespoons heavy cream
6 ounces gorgonzola cheese,
  crumbled
  Salt and pepper

1. In large sauté pan, heat 4 tablespoons (½ stick) of butter. Sauté fillets to medium-rare, about 1 minute per ounce, or until center is no longer soft to the touch but is springy. Remove and keep warm.
2. In same pan, sauté shallots. Add Port and bring to a boil. Reduce by one half.
3. Stir in cream and cheese. Reduce heat. Stir continuously until cheese has melted into sauce. Whip last 4 tablespoons butter into sauce. Serve over cooked fillets.

This is the ultimate in gourmet cheesesteaks and most appropriate for a collection of Philadelphia-based recipes. This particular cheese is strong in flavor. You may want to add the cheese slowly, using less, to taste. Or substitute a milder cheese. Wakim suggests serving it with steamed green beans and a sautéed mixture of thinly sliced carrot, zucchini and potato.

POACHED PEAR ANGLAISE

4 *Bosc pears, peeled*
3 *cups water, approximate*
½ *cup sugar*

1 *tablespoon white wine or*
lemon juice
CRÈME ANGLAISE
Chocolate syrup

1. Core pears from bottom, leaving stem at top.
2. In saucepan, bring water (to cover pears), sugar and wine to a boil. Add pears; cook 5 minutes. Drain. Cool.
3. Pool *CRÈME ANGLAISE* on plates. Swirl 2 or 3 rings of chocolate syrup over sauce. Place pear in center. Slice through sauce and chocolate rings, from center out, around pear to make a web design.

CRÈME ANGLAISE

1 *cup sugar*
8 *egg yolks*
2 *tablespoons Grand Marnier*

1 *tablespoon vanilla extract*
1½ *pints (3 cups) Half and Half*

1. In bowl, beat together sugar, yolks, Grand Marnier and vanilla.
2. In heavy saucepan, bring Half and Half to a boil; reduce heat. Gradually whip egg mixture into hot cream. Stir continuously until sugar dissolves and sauce thickens, about 4 minutes. Makes 3 cups.

Dinner for Four

Aiguillettes de Poulet Oriental

Salade de Chèvre

Médaillons de Ris de Veau aux Poireaux et Truffes

Glace de la Couverture Ivoire

Wines:

With the Salad—Touraine Rose Brut, P. Poniatowski
With the Chicken—Carmenet Sauvignon Blanc, Edna Valley
With the Sweetbreads—1979 Chateau Gruard-LaRose St. Julien

Kamol Phutlek and Cynthia Chiusa, Owners

Kamol Phutlek, Chef

Kamol Phutlek came to the United States from Thailand in 1971 to study architecture. While working in the kitchen of the prestigious La Panetiére (since closed) to pay for his schooling, he decided he'd rather work over a stove than a drafting table.

It was a decision that changed the course of food in Philadelphia forever ... not to mention Phutlek's future.

He gained further experience at Frog and LaTerrasse and studied with noted French chefs Michel Guerard (of "Cuisine Minçeur" fame) and the brothers Troisgros. Soon Phutlek had mastered the blend of Thai-French and American ingredients and techniques that led the way to a new Philadelphia-style cuisine here in much the same way that Asian and Mexican influences blended with the American on the West Coast and came to be California Cuisine. In 1980, he opened Alouette with partner Cindee Chiusa.

Relishing the freedom to create, Phutlek works from a seasonal menu with a selection of daily specials. He is constantly adapting and developing, piquing the taste buds of a devoted clientele.

"I'm using more and more Oriental ingredients now and more Japanese influences in my cooking," says Phutlek, noting the public's growing acceptance of the no longer unfamiliar foods and flavors.

This new and simpler style, says Chiusa, is perhaps best described as a blend of French with New Asian Cuisine. Representative of this extended Asian influence on Alouette's menu are such dishes as deep-fried shrimp wrapped in Nori seaweed, roast duck with tamarind sauce and black bass with a Jasmine tea cream sauce.

334 Bainbridge Street

AIGUILLETTES DE POULET ORIENTAL

2 *whole boneless chicken breasts,*
  6 ounces each
    THAI CURRY MARINADE
⅓ *cup salad oil*
⅓ *cup white vinegar*
1 *teaspoon sugar*
1 *teaspoon salt*

1 *medium carrot, julienned*
  and blanched
1 *medium cucumber, peeled,*
  halved and seeded
12 *whole scallions, trimmed*
½ *teaspoon soy sauce*
  Parsley for garnish

1. Slice chicken breasts diagonally into 16 long strips. Flatten slightly. Add to *THAI CURRY MARINADE* and coat evenly. Cover and marinate overnight. Stir occasionally.

2. At serving time, combine oil, vinegar, sugar and salt. Toss julienned carrot with half of dressing. Slice cucumber and add remaining half of dressing. Stir to coat. Set aside to marinate for 30 minutes.

3. Remove chicken from marinade; drain. Sauté strips in a non-stick pan with a few drops of oil. Brown lightly on both sides. Add scallions and soy sauce. Sauté a few minutes more. Keep warm, if necessary, before serving.

4. At the base of each of 4 plates (six o'clock), arrange 2 tablespoons each of carrot, cucumber and parsley garnish. Above salad, arrange a "fan," alternating 4 strips chicken and 3 scallions on each plate. Serve immediately.

THAI CURRY MARINADE

1 *teaspoon Thai green curry*
  paste
½ *teaspoon curry powder*
1 *teaspoon sesame oil*

2 *tablespoons soy sauce*
1 *teaspoon sugar*
¼ *cup heavy cream*

Combine all ingredients and blend thoroughly. Makes about ⅓ cup.

Thai green curry paste is the milder of two formulas from Thailand. It is available in Asian groceries and is identified by its green label.

11

SALADE DE CHÈVRE

¼ pound chèvre (goat's cheese)
1 bay leaf
1 clove garlic
2 or 3 sprigs thyme
    Olive oil
1½ cups arugula, lightly packed
1 cup julienned Belgian endive

1 cup frissé, lightly packed
1 cup radicchio, lightly packed
1 cup watercress, lightly packed
¾ cup VINAIGRETTE ALOUETTE
1 tablespoon minced chives

1. A day or more ahead, in small bowl or container, marinate cheese in a mixture of bay leaf, garlic, thyme and enough olive oil to just cover. Cover and let stand overnight. For longer periods, refrigerate.
2. When ready to assemble salad, wash all leaves carefully, drain and pat dry with clean towel.
3. Combine arugula, endive, frissé, radicchio and watercress. Toss with VINAIGRETTE ALOUETTE. Divide greens onto large serving plates.
4. Remove cheese from marinade; drain. Cut in quarters and crumble a portion over each serving of greens.

VINAIGRETTE ALOUETTE

2 tablespoons lemon juice
    Pinch each salt and pepper
¼ cup walnut oil
¼ cup salad oil

2 tablespoons red wine vinegar
2 teaspoons minced chives
2 teaspoons minced parsley

In bowl or blender, whisk together lemon juice, salt and pepper. Gradually dribble in oils while whisking. Do the same with the vinegar. Add chives and parsley. Whisk or shake well before use. Makes about ¾ cup dressing.

MÉDAILLONS DE RIS DE VEAU AUX POIREAUX ET TRUFFES

1 pair sweetbreads, about
2 pounds
Salt and pepper
Flour
1 teaspoon oil
6 tablespoons unsalted butter
1 tablespoon minced shallot
Hot pepper sauce
Lemon juice

1½ cups Port
1 cup Brown Sauce
1 piece black truffle or ½ teaspoon minced truffle peel
CREAMED LEEKS

1. To prepare sweetbreads: Place sweetbreads in bowl and set under cold, running, water for 3 hours to draw out blood. Or, cover with ice water, draining and freshening often. With a sharp knife, remove fat and membrane.

2. Put sweetbreads in saucepan, cover with cold water or vegetable bouillon and bring to a boil. Boil for 2 minutes. Reduce heat and simmer for 6 minutes. Remove and rinse under cold water.

3. Line a baking sheet or tray with a clean towel. Arrange sweetbreads on towel, and cover with another clean towel. Place another tray on top and weight with 8 to 10 pounds. Let stand, preferably refrigerated, for 3 hours.

4. When ready to serve, slice each pressed sweetbread in half horizontally. Season with salt and pepper; dust with flour. Heat oil in non-stick frypan, over high heat. Sear sweetbreads 2 to 3 minutes on each side, until crisp and slightly brown at the edge. Remove from pan, set aside and keep warm.

5. In same pan, add 4 tablespoons butter and shallots and sauté for 2 minutes. Add Port and reduce by one third. Add Brown Sauce and truffle; reduce by half. Remove from heat and stir in remaining 2 tablespoons butter. Add a dash of hot pepper sauce and lemon juice to taste.

6. Serve sweetbreads on CREAMED LEEKS.. Spoon sauce around leeks. Garnish with truffle slivers, if desired.

CREAMED LEEKS

4 large leeks
3 tablespoons unsalted butter

⅓ cup water
1⅓ cups heavy cream
Salt and pepper

1. Trim green leaves from leeks. Wash remaining white and pale green sections. Slice into quarters. Cut crosswise into ½-inch pieces and separate layers.

2. In frypan, over high heat, melt 2 tablespoons butter. Add leeks; cook for 2 minutes. Add water; cook until water evaporates.

3. Add cream and bring to a boil. Cook about 2 minutes or until cream is thick enough to coat leeks. Season with salt and pepper to taste. Add remaining 1 tablespoon butter and serve hot. Makes about 2 cups.

GLACÉ DE LA COUVERTURE IVOIRE
White Chocolate Ice Cream

2 pounds white chocolate, chopped
12 egg yolks

2 quarts (8 cups) heavy cream
1 cup sugar

1. In top of double boiler, melt chocolate until smooth.
2. In mixer bowl, beat egg yolks with sugar until thick ribbons drop from beater.
3. In saucepan, scald cream. Stir in egg-sugar mixture. Cook over low heat until mixture coats spoon.
4. Pour cream mixture into melted chocolate. Over hot water, whisk until chocolate is thoroughly blended into cream. Remove from heat and let cool 30 minutes.
5. Proceed according to directions for freezing with individual ice cream maker. Makes about 1 gallon.

This is one of Alouette's most popular dishes. Recipe may be divided for smaller portions or freezing units.

RASPBERRY SAUCE

½ pound (1 pint) fresh or frozen raspberries
½ cup sugar

½ teaspoon lemon juice
1 tablespoon orange liqueur

In blender, purée raspberries. Blend in sugar. Strain through a fine mesh sieve. Add lemon juice and orange liqueur. Chill. Serve spooned over 3 small scoops of ice cream per person or other dessert. Makes about ¾ cup.

Dinner for Six

Baked Pear and Saga Bleu Cheese Pizza
with Sour Cherries and Walnuts

Grilled Loin of Arkansas Rabbit
with Winter Greens and Herbed Risotto Salad

Grilled Gravlax of Salmon
with Beet Vinaigrette and Haricots Verts

Pink Grapefruit Cream Tarts
in Macadamia Nut Tartlette Shells

Wines:
With Pizza and Risotto—Gewurtztraminer Cuvee Ribeauville
With the Gravlax—Chardonnay Acacia, 1984
With the Tart—Franciscan Vineyards Late Harvest

Shimon and Koby Bokovza, Owners
Karyn Coigne, Executive Chef
Midi Lonergan, Pastry Chef

Our intention was to bring to Philadelphia a more cosmopolitan atmosphere," Shimon Bokovza says of Apropos, the highstyle restaurant he and his brother, Koby, opened in 1984.

"Along with the contemporary American or New Wave cuisine — whatever that means — we want people to have fun while they are here," he adds.

To that end, the open kitchen, wood-burning pizza oven and mesquite-fired grill, reinforce the sense of dinner-as-theater at Apropos. The multi-level, columned, dining room and late night entertainment clinch it. Brazilian jazz is featured at this "American bistro" on weekends.

The sleek black-lacquered look of the interior decor is complemented by a comfortable bar and a greenhouse cafe that laps out onto the sidewalk of Broad Street, the city's main thoroughfare. The restaurant serves from breakfast (brunch on Sunday) through late night daily, with pop-style pizzas and American tapas available from late afternoon until closing. A take-out pastry counter is the delight of nibblers from neighboring office buildings.

Born on the wave of California Cuisine, Apropos was fashioned in consultation with one of that foodstyle's notable proponents, Jonathan Waxman. The menu is consistently creative, sometimes unusual, always fascinating and uniquely American.

Chef Karen Coigne took over Apropos' kitchen in 1987 after training with her predecessors, Aliza Green and Derek Davis. She also worked at Jams and Arcadia in New York as part of Apropos' staff development program.

Apropos' menu is one of the most innovative in the East, with the emphasis on seasonal foods, locally produced. Freshness, the chef points out, is enforced by the intentional absense of a freezer in Apropos' kitchen.

211 South Broad Street

BAKED PEAR AND SAGA BLEU CHEESE PIZZA
WITH SOUR CHERRIES AND WALNUTS

PIZZA DOUGH
2 Bosc or Sickel pears, halved, peeled and cored
2 tablespoons butter
6 ounces Saga Bleu cheese

1 cup pitted sour cherries or a seasonal berry
2 ounces Black walnuts, halves or pieces
Mint leaves for garnish

1. During second rising of PIZZA DOUGH, assemble and prepare topping ingredients.
2. Place pear halves, cut side down, on lightly oiled baking sheet. Spot tops with butter. Place in oven and set to highest temperature, at least 500°. Bake until soft, 8 to 10 minutes. Watch carefully as some ovens heat more quickly than others. Remove. Let cool.
3. Continue preheating oven to highest temperature.
4. When PIZZA DOUGH has risen for second time, punch down and roll dough on floured surface to a 12" circle, about 1/8-inch thick. Transfer to lightly oiled pizza pan or baking sheet.
5. Arrange pear halves on top of dough. Slice or crumble cheese and distribute evenly around pears. Distribute cherries and walnuts over top.
6. Place pizza in hot oven immediately. Bake about 10 minutes or until crust is browned and cooked through. To test, lift edge of crust. Underside of dough should be firm and lightly browned. Serve garnished with mint leaves.

This recipe is adapts well to many fruits and cheeses. Lingonberries are an excellent substitute for the cherries, for instance. The chef suggests apples, gorgonzola and blueberries as one possible combination. It can work as an appetizer, entree or dessert. Served alone or after a meal, it is best paired with a red wine like Pine Ridge Merlot, Napa Valley, 1983.

PIZZA DOUGH

Lukewarm water
2 teaspoons active dry yeast
¼ cup rye flour
1 tablespoon milk
2 tablespoons olive oil
½ teaspoon salt

1 cup unbleached all-purpose flour
¾ cup bread, durum or other high-gluten flour

1. Combine ¼ cup lukewarm water, yeast and rye flour. Let stand a few minutes to soften. Stir to dissolve yeast. Let stand 20 to 30 minutes to form "sponge."

2. To the sponge, add ½ cup lukewarm water, milk, oil, salt, all-purpose and bread flours. Knead to form a smooth, elastic dough. (A mixer with dough hooks or a processor may be used to knead dough. Follow directions with machine.)

3. Cover dough and let rise, draft-free, for 1 hour. Punch dough down and let rise again for 30 minutes or until doubled. Use as directed in recipe. Makes dough for one 12-inch pizza.

GRILLED LOIN OF ARKANSAS RABBIT
WITH WINTER GREENS AND HERBED RISOTTO SALAD

1 dressed rabbit, 3 to 4 pounds
5 teaspoons Dijon mustard
2 tablespoons chopped fresh rosemary
2 tablespoons extra-virgin olive oil
Zest of 2 limes
Salt and fresh ground pepper

1 pound mixed seasonal greens (arugula, endive, kale, raddichio, red chard, spinach or others)
2 teaspoons Balsamic vinegar
HERBED RISOTTO SALAD
12 or 18 baby carrots with tops, blanched

1. Remove the bones from both whole rib loins (2 to 3 ounces each) of rabbit, or have your butcher do this for you. Use carcass to make rabbit stock as you would Chicken Stock. (Legs may be reserved, if desired, and grilled or roasted like chicken.)

2. Spread loins with mixture of mustard, rosemary, 1 teaspoon olive oil, lime zest, salt and pepper to taste. Set aside to marinate at least 30 minutes. (This can be done ahead and refrigerated.)

3. When ready to serve, remove excess marinade and grill rabbit loins or sauté in olive oil 6 to 10 minutes. Timing will vary with thickness. Rabbit should be cooked to medium and will feel firm to the touch.

4. Meanwhile, toss greens with remaining olive oil and Balsamic vinegar. Arrange greens on large serving plates, making sure to accentuate the colors and variety. Garnish each plate with 2 or 3 baby carrots. Spoon HERBED RISOTTO SALAD in center of greens.

5. Slice rabbit loins into small medallions or diagonal scallops. Arrange 2 or 3 slices on top of each portion of risotto. Serve immediately.

For those disinclined to use rabbit, a chicken breast might be substituted, or omit the meat if you wish.

HERBED RISOTTO SALAD

1 large onion, diced
2 tablespoons extra-virgin olive oil
½ pound arborio rice (a mounded cup) rabbit or Chicken Stock, about 3 cups, heated

2 tablespoons chopped fresh rosemary
Juice of 2 limes, about 4 tablespoons

1. In heavy saucepan, sauté onion in 1 tablespoon olive oil until translucent. Add rice and sauté for 1 minute. Add 1 cup hot stock and simmer over low heat, stirring frequently, until liquid is absorbed. As liquid is absorbed, gradually add more stock, one ladle or about ¼ cup at a time until rice is cooked through but slightly chewy, about 20 minutes. Do not cook rice dry between additions. Remove from heat while still moist.

2. Spread risotto on tray to cool. Add 1 tablespoon olive oil, rosemary and lime juice. Stir to distribute dressing. Serve at room temperature. Makes 3 cups.

GRILLED GRAVLAX OF SALMON
WITH BEET VINAIGRETTE AND HARICOTS VERTS

2 salmon fillets, about 1½
  pounds each
½ cup kosher or coarse sea salt
½ cup granulated sugar
1 tablespoon black peppercorns,
  cracked
5 bay leaves

¾ cup chopped fresh herbs
  (basil, chervil, chives,
  coriander, fennel, marjoram,
  tarragon, thyme and/or
  parsley)
1 pound haricots verts or other
  crisp green beans, blanched
4 tablespoons butter
  BEET VINAIGRETTE

1. A day or more ahead, combine salt, sugar, pepper, bay leaves and herbs. Spread herb mixture evenly over flesh side of 1 fillet. Place second fillet, reversing thin end to thick, flesh side down over fillet with herbs. Place between towels or wrap in foil. Weight top. Refrigerate 24 hours for light cure. Longer curing gives stronger flavor and more fully "cooks" the fish. (For Gravlax that needs no cooking, cure fish 3 to 4 days, until translucent and firm.)

2. When ready, scrape off seasonings. Refrigerate until ready to serve. Slicing on the diagonal, spacing cuts about ¾-inch on fillet, cut broad, thin, slices from flesh side of fillet. Grill salmon slices lightly on each side, just to warm fish through and mark surface. Salmon should remain reddish or "rare" looking in center.

3. Sauté blanched green beans lightly in butter.

4. For each serving, spoon BEET VINAIGRETTE onto plate and arrange two slices of salmon on sauce. Portion green beans on the side. Garnish with tarragon, if desired.

If filleting whole salmon, cut fish behind gill and slip knife flat along bone. Rub flesh to raise any small bones. Remove with fish tweezer. Trim fat after curing. Davis also suggests that, when the salmon is gone, the skin may be cut in thin strips, julienne-style, and fried in hot oil to make fish cracklings for garnish.

BEET VINAIGRETTE

2 medium beets, preferably
  yellow, peeled and cut up
2 shallots, peeled
¾ cup extra virgin olive oil

3 tablespoons champagne
  vinegar
2 sprigs of tarragon
  Salt and white pepper, to
  taste

1. Boil beets in water to cover until very soft, 15 to 20 minutes.
2. In blender, combine cooked beets, shallots, olive oil and vinegar. Purée at high speed until emulsified. Season to taste with salt and pepper. Makes about 1½ cups.

PINK GRAPEFRUIT CREAM TARTS
IN MACADAMIA NUT TARTLETTE SHELLS

8 pink grapefruit
1½ cups granulated sugar
6 egg yolks
¼ pound (1 stick) unsalted
  butter
1 pint (2 cups) heavy cream
6 or 8 MACADAMIA NUT TARTLETTE
  SHELLS

CHOCOLATE CITRUS SAUCE
CANDIED GRAPEFRUIT PEEL,
for garnish
Additional whole macadamia
nuts, for garnish
Mint leaves, for garnish

1. At least one day ahead, remove rinds from 4 grapefruit, cutting from pole to pole, in 1-inch to 1½-inch wide strips. Use for CANDIED GRAPEFRUIT PEEL.
2. Grate or zest the rinds of remaining 4 grapefruit; set aside. Squeeze juice from 7 grapefruit, leaving 1 whole for garnish segments.
3. Over moderate-low heat, in a stainless steel or non-aluminum saucepan, reduce juice by one half, about 30 minutes. Remove from heat. Cool to room temperature.

4. In stainless steel saucepan or bowl, over simmering water, beat sugar with egg yolks. Stir in juice concentrate and grated rind. Stir frequently with wooden spoon, adding butter one tablespoon at a time as curd thickens. Cook mixture until very thick. Strain through a fine sieve.*

5. On day of serving, whip heavy cream to soft peaks and fold into grapefruit curd. Pipe or spoon grapefruit cream into MACADAMIA NUT TARTLETTE SHELLS. Makes enough for up to 20 individual (3½-inch) tarts or 2 large (12-inch) tarts.

6. Garnish tarts with CANDIED GRAPEFRUIT PEEL, whole macadamia nuts and mint leaves. Serve with CHOCOLATE CITRUS SAUCE to the side. Fillet grapefruit sections, slice thin and fan on sauce.

* Prepared curd will keep, refrigerated, for two weeks.

This recipe makes about 20 individual or 2 large tarts. Halve recipe or hold half of curd and pastry for later use.

MACADAMIA NUT TARTLETTE SHELLS

½ pound (2 sticks) unsalted butter, at room temperature
¼ cup granulated sugar
1 large egg, beaten
1 teaspoon vanilla extract

1 teaspoon almond extract
½ teaspoon ground cinnamon
3 cups all-purpose flour
10 ounces macadamia nuts, chopped fine

1. Cream together butter and sugar just until blended. Add beaten egg, vanilla and almond extracts, and cinnamon. Stir in flour and chopped nuts to form a soft dough.

2. Divide and press evenly into tart pans. Makes enough for about 20 individual (3½-inch) tarts or 2 large (12-inch) tarts. Freeze unused dough or bake as cookies.

3. Chill 30 minutes; bake at 350° for 12 to 15 minutes or until golden. Let cool before filling.

CHOCOLATE CITRUS SAUCE

1 cup heavy cream
6 ounces semisweet chocolate,
   chopped or in bits

1 ounce (2 tablespoons) orange
liqueur
Juice of ½ grapefruit, about
¼ cup

1. In heavy saucepan, heat cream and chocolate pieces. Stir until chocolate is melted.
2. Add orange liqueur and grapefruit juice. Remove from heat. Serve warm with PINK GRAPEFRUIT CREAM TARTS or other dessert, as desired. Makes about 2 cups.

CANDIED GRAPEFRUIT PEEL

1 cup water
1 cup sugar

Rind of 4 grapefruit, cut in
wide strips
Additional sugar

1. In saucepan, combine water and sugar; bring to a boil. Whisk to dissolve sugar.
2. Meanwhile, remove white membrane from inside of rinds, leaving just the thinnest layer.
3. Drop rind into boiling syrup. Turn off heat. Let rind stand in hot syrup for 24 hours, until translucent.
4. Remove rind from syrup; drain. Square off the strips of rind and slice into ¹⁄₁₆-inch julienne strips.
5. Roll julienned rind in sugar, shaking off excess. Store in airtight container. Use for garnish.

AT THE LATHAM

Dinner for Six

Chanterelles with Capellini

Zucchini Curry Soup

Quackling Salad

Medallions of Wild Boar with Jack Daniel's Sauce and Baked Granny Smith Apples

White Chocolate Praliné Mousse

Wine:

Rutherford Hill Merlot

Eli Karetny, Owner
Wayne Marks, General Manager
Gerald A. Dougherty, Chef

B ogart's brings a little bit of Casablanca to Center City. Located off the lobby in The Latham Hotel, the cozy café is North African in décor, recalling Rick's Bar in the Humphrey Bogart film classic. But the food is all-American.

The menu draws on both traditional and contemporary tastes and cooking styles for dishes that provide diners with a sense of security (a 20-ounce porterhouse steak, ribs, mixed grill, lobster, and the like) while offering invention and a selection of New American cuisine dishes. In addition, manager/maitre d' Wayne Marks specializes in tableside food preparation including classics like Caesar salad, steak Diane and bananas Foster.

"Bogart's has always been a popular place for meeting and eating," says owner Eli Karetny. "Now we've moved to a new level of food, wine and service."

Opened in 1970 as a privately operated adjunct to the new hotel, Bogart's quickly became a popular gathering spot in a city hungry for good food and new settings. When Karetny acquired the restaurant in 1977, the transition from old-style hotel dining room to respected restaurant began. All the while, Bogart's has continued to serve three meals a day, seven days a week.

The addition of chef Gerald Dougherty in 1986 brought the kitchen still closer to Karetny's ideal.

"Gerald brings a wealth of skill and artistry to Bogart's," says Karetny, who monitors the menu as closely as the business. "He creates exciting food with American ingredients and has a very real flair for preparing beautiful food."

17th and Walnut Streets

CHANTERELLES WITH CAPELLINI

½ *pound fresh capellini*
1½ *pounds Chanterelles*
¼ *cup* CLARIFIED BUTTER
½ *teaspoon minced shallot*

6 *tablespoons* BROWN SAUCE
6 *tablespoons Madeira*
6 *tablespoons butter*
Salt and pepper

1. Cook capellini in boiling water until barely tender, 3 minutes. Strain and keep warm over the water.
2. In large skillet, sauté Chanterelles in CLARIFIED BUTTER for 2 minutes. Add shallots; cook 2 minutes more.
3. Add BROWN SAUCE and Madeira; reduce until almost dry. Stir in whole butter, in pieces. Add salt and pepper to taste.
4. Return capellini to hot water to reheat, 1 minute. Drain. Toss with mushrooms. Serve.

CLARIFIED BUTTER

To Clarify Butter: Melt butter, skimming off any foam. Strain off clear yellow oil, discarding milky residue. Or leave butter in a stainless steel bowl in a 200° oven for 1 hour. Skim crust. Chill. Unmold and scrape residue from base. Cover; refrigerate. Clear butter withstands higher heat.

BROWN SAUCE

5 *pounds veal bones or*
  knuckles, broken
3 *carrots*
3 *large onions*
2 *stalks celery*
1 *leek*
8 *ripe tomatoes or ½ cup*
  purée or
  3 *tablespoons paste*

1 *bunch parsley, 2 to 3 ounces*
1 *tablespoon thyme*
3 *bay leaves*
10 *peppercorns*
2 *gallons cold water*

1. Spread bones in baking pan. Cut carrots, onions, celery and leek into pan. Brown in 450° oven, 45 minutes.
2. In stockpot, combine browned bones and vegetables, tomatoes, parsley, thyme, bay and peppercorns with water. Cook below boiling for 5 hours. Skim surface occasionally.
3. Strain stock, discarding bones and pulp.
4. Continue reduction to 2½ quarts (10 cups).

The progression of classic brown sauces starts with a basic vegetable-flavored brown meat stock. With substantial reduction, a slight roux thickening and additional flavors (typically tomato and Madeira, often ham), a Brown Sauce is produced. More hours of cooking turn that Brown Sauce into the thicker Demi-Glace sauce base used in fine restaurants. This Brown Sauce shortcuts the process by overlapping the steps for stock and sauce, without a roux. If desired, add a browned butter/flour thickener after straining. These bases take time, but need only casual attention. While a restaurant may have huge stock pots brewing around the clock, the home cook can freeze sauce base in recipe portions to have on hand when needed for weeks ahead.

ZUCCHINI CURRY SOUP

½ cup chopped onion	6 cups CHICKEN STOCK
½ cup chopped apple	6 tablespoons CURRY BLEND
4 tablespoons CLARIFIED BUTTER	1 ripe banana
6 cups zucchini, thinly sliced (8 medium to 12 small)	1 cup heavy cream Salt and pepper

1. In saucepan, sauté onion and apple in butter until soft. Add zucchini. Cook until mushy. Drain off liquid. Add CHICKEN STOCK, CURRY BLEND, banana and cream. Bring to a boil. Season to taste.
2. Purée soup in batches in blender or processor. If desired, serve with shredded zucchini or fan of thin slices.

CHICKEN STOCK

4 pounds chicken carcasses or
  necks
1 leek, chopped
1 onion, chopped
1 stalk celery, chopped

1 bunch parsley (2 to 3 ounces)
2 teaspoons thyme
3 bay leaves
5 quarts cold water

1. In stockpot, combine all ingredients and bring to a boil. Reduce heat and simmer for 2 hours. Skim surface occasionally.
2. Strain. Makes about 3 quarts.

CURRY BLEND

2 tablespoons coriander
2 teaspoons tumeric
2 teaspoons black pepper

1½ teaspoons cayenne pepper
1 teaspoon cardamon
1 teaspoon cumin

In spice grinder or with mortar and pestle, grind all ingredients. Or combine pre-ground spices. Makes ¼ cup.

QUACKLING SALAD

1 duckling, quartered, boned*
  Salt and pepper
1½ pounds spinach leaves

¼ cup raspberry vinegar
½ pint raspberries
1 cup QUACKLINGS

1. Preheat oven to 450°.
2. Score skin on duck breast and thighs. Season with salt and pepper. Sear duck, skin side down, in skillet. Transfer to oven; roast for 8 to 10 minutes, to medium rare. Remove breast and leg meat. Reserve skin for cracklings, fat for dressing and carcass for stock.
3. Wash spinach; drain and pat dry. Divide on plates.

4. Slice duck meat thinly on the diagonal and divide on salads. Mix ½ cup hot duck fat with vinegar and drizzle over salads.

5. Divide QUACKLINGS on salad. Ring with raspberries.

* To bone duckling: Run knife down center of breast bone and work along bone to release meat. Detach leg bone at bottom of thigh. Slit meat down center and release thigh bone.

QUACKLINGS

To make Duck Quacklings: Cut roasted duck skin in thin strips. Render in saucepan over medium heat for 10 to 15 minutes, until crisp and brown, draining fat periodically.

MEDALLIONS OF WILD BOAR WITH JACK DANIEL'S SAUCE

2 pounds boneless loin of boar or pork
Seasoned flour
¼ pound (1 stick) unsalted butter
3 shallots, minced

1 Granny Smith apple, peeled, cored and minced
½ cup Jack Daniel's whiskey
3 cups DEMI-GLACE
2 tablespoons minced parsley
Salt and pepper
BAKED GRANNY SMITH APPLES

1. Slice loin into 12 medallions; flatten slightly. Dredge in seasoned flour. Sauté meat in 4 tablespoons butter, 2 minutes on each side. Remove; keep warm.

2. Add shallots, chopped apple and whiskey. Flame to burn off alcohol. Reduce to ¼ cup. Add DEMI-GLACE and reduce by one half. Add parsley; season to taste. Finish by stirring in remaining 4 tablespoons butter.

3. Return medallions to sauce; cook through. Serve 2 medallions per person with BAKED GRANNY SMITH APPLE garnish.

DEMI-GLACE

8 cups Brown Sauce   2 cups Madeira

In heavy saucepan, combine Brown Sauce and Madeira. Simmer gently, reducing to 3 cups of thick sauce base, 2 to 3 hours. Reduce heat; stir often as sauce thickens.

BAKED GRANNY SMITH APPLES

3 Granny Smith Apples   2 tablespoons butter
2 tablespoons brown sugar

Core and halve apples. Sprinkle each cut surface with 1 teaspoon brown sugar. Dot with 1 teaspoon butter. Broil about 10 minutes until tender. Serve as garnish.

WHITE CHOCOLATE PRALINÉ MOUSSE

¼ cup sugar
½ cup chopped pecans
1 pound white chocolate, chopped
4 cups heavy cream

¼ cup white cream of cacao liqueur
1 teaspoon vanilla extract
Whole pecans for garnish

1. In sauté pan, melt sugar. Stir over medium heat until sugar begins to brown. Quickly stir in pecans to coat. Turn onto waxed paper; spread thin. Cool. Crush.
2. Over hot water, melt chocolate with ¼ cup of cream, liqueur and vanilla. Set over ice. Whip to soft peaks, adding remaining cream 1 cup at a time. Watch closely. If overbeaten, mousse gets grainy and ultimately breaks down.
3. Fold crushed pecans into chocolate mixture; chill 1 hour. Serve with pecan garnish. Makes ½ gallon.

Dinner for Eight

Acadian Crabmeat Tart with Creole Béarnaise Sauce

Seasonal Greens with Almond Garlic Dressing

Cajun Seafood on a Fried Eggplant Plank

Red Pepper Mousse

Chocolate Praliné Swirl Cake

Wine:

Gundlach-Bundschu Gerwurtztraminer, 1984

Bill Curry and Judy DeVicaris, Owners
John Barrett, Chef
Terry Thompson, Menu Consultant

Cafe Nola takes its name from the city that gave it soul, the home of Cajun-Creole cuisine, New Orleans. Opened in 1981, well before the craving for Cajun and the run on redfish set American tongues (and skillets) to burning, Nola continues to set a high standard for a regional foodstyle that in less caring kitchens, less skilled hands, can defeat even cast-iron stomachs.

When partners Bill Curry, a former newspaper columnist, and Judy DeVicaris, an interior decorator, first conceived Cafe Nola, they wanted a "fun" restaurant that would fit into Philadelphia's festive South Street neighborhood. Sensing the same Bohemian feeling here that has made the French Quarter a mecca for lovers of food and fun, they sought to capture the flavors as well. They succeeded.

Despite the sometimes heavy use of hot peppers and spices, says Chef John Barrett, "it is onions, bell peppers and celery that are basic to Cajun-Creole cooking. They are the Holy Trinity in all sauces." A graduate of the Culinary Institute of America, Barrett works closely with menu consultant Terry Thompson, author of *Cajun-Creole Cooking* (HP Books), to perfect dishes. Thompson became Nola's Cajun-Creole conscience in 1983.

Because both New Orleans and Philadelphia experienced mass immigration from Italy around the turn of the century, some dishes reflect the Italian influence on Creole cooking. And each fall, Nola celebrates its own Creole-Italia Fest by featuring dishes that marry the two cuisines.

"Like the New Orleans area, we have good resources of seafood," says Curry. "For specials, we try to be creative within the framework of basic Cajun-Creole cooking, like adding clams and mussels to the Jambalaya."

Nola's heart, however, remains with authentic New Orleans fare, using fresh crawfish, redfish and heads-on shrimp flown in from the Gulf. An oyster bar greets guests on the way to the Venetian-mirrored "Veranda" dining room.

The Curry-DeVicaris flair for combining food and fun extends to their other eateries, Copabanana at 4th and South Streets and Copa, Too! at 263 South 15th Street.

328 South Street

ACADIAN CRABMEAT TARTS
WITH CREOLE BÉARNAISE SAUCE

4 tablespoons butter
8 scallions, finely chopped,
   including green tops
¼ cup finely chopped bell
   pepper

1 pound backfin lump
   crabmeat
8 pre-baked individual tart
   shells, see TART PASTRY
   CREOLE BÉARNAISE SAUCE

1. In heavy 12" skillet, over medium heat, melt butter. Sauté scallions and pepper 3 to 5 minutes until crisp-tender. Add crabmeat; toss quickly, but gently, just to heat through. Do not break up lumps. Set aside; keep warm.

2. Place tart shells on baking sheet. Warm and re-crisp in 350° oven for up to 5 minutes, as needed. Meanwhile prepare CREOLE BÉARNAISE SAUCE, recipe below.

3. To Assemble Tarts: Place 1 tart shell on each appetizer plate, fill generously with crabmeat. Top with 2 tablespoons hot CREOLE BÉARNAISE SAUCE. Serve at once.

TART PASTRY
(Food Processor)

1 cup all-purpose unbleached
   flour
1 stick frozen unsalted butter,
   cut in 1" chunks

Pinch of salt
3 to 4 tablespoons ice water

1. Place flour, butter and salt in work bowl of food processor fitted with steel blade. Pulse On- Off, until butter is cut into pea-sized pieces. With machine running, gradually add ice water through feed tube just to moisten dough. Do NOT process to form a ball.

2. Turn mixture onto work surface, bringing dough together with hands and pastry scraper. Do not overwork. Wrap in plastic; refrigerate 30 minutes before rolling.

3. On lightly floured work surface, roll dough in one direction only to a thickness of ¹⁄₁₆". Pastry should be extra thin for tart cups. (For pie crust, roll pastry to ⅛".) Loosely roll pastry around rolling pin and unroll onto pan of 3" tart shells. With sharp knife, cut pastry between cups of tart pan. Let pastry fall into place, patting lightly into tart shapes. Prick bottom of pastry with fork.

   NOTE: To reduce shrinkage in baking, be careful not to stretch pastry when fitting molds. Freeze pastry shells for 15 minutes before baking to further reduce shrinkage.

4. To pre-bake pastry shells, line with a round piece of foil. Add a layer of dry beans, rice or metal pie weights. Bake in preheated 400° oven for 15 minutes. Carefully remove foil and weights. Bake shells 5 minutes more, until golden. Makes up to 12 tart shells or pastry for a single-crust pie.

CREOLE BÉARNAISE SAUCE

2 tablespoons minced scallions, including tops
1 tablespoon fresh tarragon or 1½ teaspoons dried
1 tablespoon fresh chervil or 1½ teaspoons dried
1 tablespoon minced shallots
¼ teaspoon salt
¼ teaspoon freshly ground black pepper
3 cloves garlic, minced

Juice of ½ lemon
¼ cup dry white wine
4 drops liquid red pepper sauce (Tabasco), or to taste
3 egg yolks
½ teaspoon cayenne pepper, or to taste
2 teaspoons Creole mustard (Zatarain) or spicy Dijon
¼ pound (1 stick) unsalted butter, melted

1. In heavy saucepan, over medium-high heat, combine scallions, tarragon, chervil, shallots, salt, black pepper, garlic, lemon juice, wine and red pepper sauce. Cook until liquid is reduced to about 1 tablespoon. Remove from heat; set aside.

2. In heavy saucepan, over low heat, or in top of double-boiler, combine egg yolks, cayenne and mustard. Whisk briskly until yolks thicken and turn a light lemon yellow. Remove from heat and rapidly whisk in the reduced wine-herb mixture.

3. Return pan to low heat and very slowly whisk in melted butter. Remove from heat. Whisk another minute or two until sauce is smooth and glossy. If desired, strain sauce through fine strainer or doubled cheesecloth. If a thinner sauce is desired, add up to 1 tablespoon additional lemon juice. Makes about 1 cup.

The strength and flavor of red pepper sauces vary with different brands. Measurements for pepper sauce are based on the stronger blends.

SEASONAL GREENS WITH ALMOND-GARLIC DRESSING

*1½ to 2 pounds mixed salad greens
(red and green leaf lettuce,
romaine or other greens)*

ALMOND-GARLIC DRESSING

In large bowl, toss torn greens lightly with *ALMOND-GARLIC DRESSING.* Serve in 3 to 4 ounce portions.

ALMOND-GARLIC DRESSING

¼ cup slivered almonds,
    toasted
½ cup red wine vinegar
1 teaspoon salt

½ teaspoon freshly ground
    black pepper, or to taste
¾ cup olive oil
3 small cloves garlic, peeled

In blender or food processor, combine toasted almonds, vinegar, salt and pepper. With machine running, add garlic and drizzle oil though center cap or feed tube. Store dressing in container with tight-fitting lid; refrigerate. Makes about 1¼ cups.

To toast slivered almonds, brown lightly in a hot skillet with 1 tablespoon butter or spread on pan in hot oven, 375° to 400°, for 8 to 10 minutes.

CAJUN SEAFOOD ON A FRIED EGGPLANT PLANK

2 or 3 eggplants, 1 to 1½
    pounds each, unpeeled
    Salt
2 cups yellow cornmeal
.1½ teaspoons sugar
1½ teaspoons cayenne pepper
1½ teaspoons salt
1½ teaspoons freshly ground
    black pepper
    All-purpose flour

2 eggs beaten with 2
    tablespoons milk
    Peanut oil for deep-frying
    CAJUN SEAFOOD SAUCE
    Parsley sprigs for garnish
    Lemon wedges dipped
    in cayenne pepper

1. Cut eggplant in 8 lengthwise slices, ½" to ¾" thick. Spread slices on sheet trays; sprinkle with salt. Place weighted tray on top. Let stand at least 45 minutes to draw out bitterness.

2. In large bowl, stir together cornmeal, sugar, cayenne, salt and black pepper. Set aside.

3. When ready to cook, remove pressed eggplant and pat dry with paper towels. Dredge each slice in flour, coating well. Dip each slice in egg-milk wash. Dredge in reserved, seasoned cornmeal. Coat both sides well, shaking off excess.*

4. Heat oil to 365° and deep fry eggplant slices, a few at a time, until coating is crisp and golden brown. Drain on paper towels. Keep warm until all slices are fried.

5. When ready to serve, place a slice of fried eggplant on each plate and top with about 1 cup CAJUN SEAFOOD SAUCE. Serve hot. Garnish each plate with parsley and a lemon wedge, the center edge of which has been dipped in cayenne pepper.

* Eggplant can be prepared to this point several hours ahead and refrigerated until ready to cook.

CAJUN SEAFOOD SAUCE

1 large eggplant, peeled
4 tablespoons (½ stick) unsalted butter
1 medium onion, chopped
1 green bell pepper, cored and chopped
1 large rib celery, finely chopped
1 large clove garlic, minced
2 tablesoons minced parsley
½ teaspoon cayenne pepper
½ teaspoon freshly ground black pepper
½ teaspoon white pepper
½ teaspoon dried basil
½ teaspoon dried oregano
¼ teaspoon dried thyme

¾ teaspoon liquid red pepper sauce (Tabasco), or to taste
¼ cup all-purpose flour
½ cup ajun sseafood stock or clam juice
½ teaspoon salt or to taste
16 large or 24 medium shrimp, about 1 pound, peeled and deveined
¾ pound peeled crawfish tails with fat (rock shrimp may be substituted out of season)
½ pound lump crabmeat
½ pound redfish, in 1" cubes
½ cup chopped scallion

1. Cut eggplant in 1" cubes. In large saucepan, cover eggplant with water and cook until tender, about 7 minutes. Drain thoroughly; purée eggplant; set aside.
2. In heavy saucepan, melt butter. Over medium-low heat, add onion, bell pepper, celery, garlic, parsley, cayenne, black pepper, white pepper, basil, oregano, thyme and red pepper sauce. Cook slowly, stirring, until vegetables are very soft, about 15 minutes.
3. Sift in flour gradually; stir well to blend. Increase heat; cook, stirring, for 5 minutes.
4. Stir in reserved, pureed eggplant. Add CAJUN SEAFOOD STOCK. Cook, stirring, until thickened. Add salt. Adjust seasonings to taste.*
5. Add shrimp to hot sauce; cook about 3 minutes. When shrimp start to turn opaque, add crawfish tails with fat and redfish. Cook, stirring gently, until fish flesh becomes opaque. Gently stir in crabmeat, being careful not to break up lumps. Cook 1 minute. If sauce is too thick, thin with up to ¼ cup additional CAJUN SEAFOOD STOCK. Stir in scallions. Makes about 10 cups.

* Sauce can be prepared to this point up to 36 hours ahead and refrigerated until ready to assemble.

CAJUN SEAFOOD STOCK

1 pound seafood shells and/or fish bones (no heads)
½ onion, unpeeled
2 tablespoons chopped celery
1 small clove garlic, crushed
1 wedge lemon
1 tablespoon shrimp and crab boil seasoning
6 whole cloves
6 black peppercorns

1. In stockpot, combine shells, onion, celery, garlic, lemon, shrimp and crab boil, cloves and peppercorns. Add 5" water to cover. Over high heat, bring to a full boil. Skim surface of stock.

2. Reduce heat; simmer for about 3 hours or until liquid is reduced by half. Strain stock; refrigerate or freeze. Makes 1 quart strong stock.

This is a spicy hot stock, greenish-brown in color, and imparts a distinct taste to the dishes for which it is used. No substitute is truly comparable.

RED PEPPER MOUSSE

6 *tablespoons (¾ stick)*
unsalted butter
8 *red bell peppers, seeded and*
coarsely chopped

2 *large eggs, lightly beaten*
1 *cup heavy cream*

1. Melt butter in saucepan over low heat. Add peppers and cook, covered, over very low heat for 30 to 40 minutes until very tender. Cook slowly to avoid sticking and a burned, bitter taste.
2. Drain cooked peppers thoroughly and pass through the fine blade of a food mill. (Processor or blender may be used but will not remove skin from purée, leaving a sharper taste. Strain, if desired.)
3. Add eggs and heavy cream to purée; blend well. Divide between 8 well-buttered, individual dariole molds or 3" custard cups.
4. Set molds in baking pan. Add warm water to pan halfway up sides of molds. Bake at 375° for 20 minutes or until mousse is set and center is not sticky when lightly touched. Mousse will hold in water bath, in warm oven, for up to 1 hour. When ready to serve, remove from oven and unmold immediately onto serving plates.

CHOCOLATE PRALINÉ SWIRL CAKE

CAKE:
9 *eggs, separated*
¾ *cup superfine sugar*
1 *tablespoon vanilla extract*
cup ground pecans
¾ *teaspoon cream of tartar*
¼ *A pinch of salt*
¾ *cup Dutch processed cocoa*
(preferably Droste)
14 *ounces soft almond paste*
(as Odense)
Confectioners' sugar
¾ *cup Amaretto or praline*
liqueur

CHOCOLATE FILLING:
28 *ounces bittersweet chocolate*
(Cacao Barry or other good
quality chocolate made
without parafin)
3 *tablespoons unsalted butter*
1 *quart (4 cups) heavy cream,*
at room temperature
½ *pound PECAN PRALINÉ,*
crumbled

1. Line a 10"x15"x1" jelly roll pan with lightly-buttered parchment or waxed paper.
2. In mixing bowl, beat egg yolks, sugar and vanilla until pale yellow. Fold in ground pecans.
3. In separate bowl, beat egg whites with cream of tartar and salt until soft peaks form. Fold ¼ of whipped whites into yolk mixture. Gently fold in remaining whites.
4. Turn batter into prepared pan, spreading evenly. Bake at 350° about 25 minutes or until cake is springy to the touch.
5. Meanwhile, on work surface, knead ½ cup of cocoa into almond paste. Dust work surface with remaining ¼ cup of cocoa and roll almond paste into a 9"x14" rectangle. Refrigerate.
6. Dust towel or pastry cloth with confectioners' sugar. Turn cake out onto cloth; remove paper liner. Trim ½" from all sides of cake.
7. Place chilled almond paste on hot cake. Roll cake up lengthwise like jelly roll. Cool completely.

8. Pour liqueur into shallow plate. With sharp knife, cut cake roll into slices about ⅓″ thick. (You will need 31 perfect slices.) Dip one side of each slice briefly into liqueur. Cover bottom of 10″ springform pan with cake slices, liqueur side down, working from a ring of 12 slices around edge, to an inner ring of 6, to a single slice in center. Press firmly. Place remaining slices upright against sides of pan, pressing firmly. Refrigerate.

9. To prepare filling, melt chocolate and butter in top of double boiler or in large stainless steel mixing bowl set over barely simmering water. Stir until smooth. Remove from heat.

10. If using double boiler, transfer chocolate to large mixing bowl. Fold in heavy cream, 1 cup at a time, just until combined. Fold in crumbled PECAN PRALINÉ. Pour into cake-lined pan. Cover and refrigerate overnight.

11. Invert chilled cake onto serving platter. Remove springform pan. Serve with whipped cream, if desired. Makes 12 servings.

Cake can be prepared in stages over a period of one or more days in advance of serving.

PECAN PRALINÉ

¾ cup white sugar	A pinch of salt
¾ cup brown sugar	2 tablespoons unsalted butter
½ cup milk	½ teaspoon vanilla extract
¼ teaspoon cream of tartar	1¼ cups pecan halves

1. In saucepan, over medium-high heat, combine white and brown sugars, milk, cream of tartar and salt. Cook until candy thermometer reaches 238°.

2. Remove from heat and cool to 220°. Add butter and vanilla. Stir briskly until thick and creamy. Stir in pecans.

3. Spread on buttered parchment or waxed paper. Let cool until hard. Break into pieces. Makes about 1 pound, enough for 2 cakes.

This recipe is designed for use in the Chocolate Praline Cake and differs slightly from recipes for clear Praline candy.

Dinner for Six

Chicken Liver Pâté with Peppercorns and Cognac

Potato-Leek Soup

Belgian Endive, Apple, Roquefort and Hazelnut Salad
with Raspberry Hazelnut Vinaigrette

Carambola Champagne Sorbet

Sautéed Breast of Chicken with Shiitake Mushrooms
and Whole Grain Mustard Cream Sauce

Timbales of Broccoli, Cauliflower and Carrot

Dauphine Potatoes

Grand Marnier Chocolate Truffle Tart

Wine:

Gewurztraminer, Hugel, 1983

Ron and Lisa Kinzinger, Proprietors
Ron Kinzinger, Chef

47

THE COLEBROOKDALE INN

Much of the Victorian-era charm of The Colebrookdale Inn is the result of remodeling done in 1981. But at least as much of the mood and French country farmhouse feeling here comes from Ron and Lisa Kinzinger, the young couple who bought the property in 1984. For Ron, a native of nearby Sellersville, Pa., and a graduate of the Culinary Institute of America, it was the fulfillment of a dream.

"Lisa has a real estate license and sold restaurants. When she found this one for sale, we bought it," says Kinzinger, who had been executive chef in charge of three popular restaurants in Bloomingdale's King of Prussia store before striking out on his own.

Located on the outskirts of Boyertown, in between Pottstown and Reading, Colebrookdale is near enough antique shops and farmers' markets for a full day in the country. Diners frequently make the 40-mile drive northwest from Philadelphia just to enjoy an intimate, elegant weeknight dinner.

The food and mood is French but the interpretation of classic cuisine is Kinzinger's own. He makes use of flavorful touches like lobster butter or roquefort butter accents for tournedos, honey-lime sauce with duck and tomato-basil cream sauce on scallops. For attention to detail alone, The Colebrookdale Inn is unmatched. A garnish of tiny, filled, quail egg cups accompanies the paté. Flavored butters are served with hot-from-the-oven, crusty French rolls. A refreshing sorbet preceeds the entrée. Every dish is "picture perfect," with a taste to match.

"I have this philosophy that if it's strainable, strain it," says Kinzinger. "It makes everything a little bit finer."

Farmington Avenue
Village of Colebrookdale

CHICKEN LIVER PÂTÉ WITH PEPPERCORNS AND COGNAC

½ cup celery tops
12 black peppercorns
3 bay leaves
6 tablespoons (¾ stick) unsalted butter
½ cup finely chopped Spanish onion
¼ teaspoon minced garlic

1 teaspoon dried thyme
1 pound chicken livers
4 tablespoon cognac
½ teaspoon ground allspice
¼ teaspoon salt
2 tablespoons green peppercorns, drained and divided
¼ cup heavy cream

1. Tie celery, peppercorns and bay in cheesecloth bag and simmer in saucepan with 2 quarts water for 15 minutes.
2. In sauté pan, melt butter. Add onion, garlic and thyme. Cook, covered, over low heat until onion is limp and lightly colored (yellow), about 15 minutes.
3. Trim all fat from livers. Add to seasoned water. Poach, barely simmering, for 10 minutes. Do not overcook. Livers should be pale pink inside. Discard water and herbs.
4. Combine livers and onions in processor or blender. Add cognac, allspice, salt, and 4 teaspoons green peppercorns. Process until very smooth, scraping down sides.
5. Add cream; pulse blend just to incorporate.
6. Transfer to bowl. Stir in remaining 2 teaspoons green peppercorns. Cover closely with plastic wrap to keep air from surface. Chill 6 hours. Serve small scoops or pack into crock for dip. Makes about 2 cups. May be made 1 day ahead.

Kinzinger arranges dark pumpernickel rounds, cornichons, niçoise olives, a tomato crown and quail egg crowns filled with chopped egg yolk and diced onion around 2 oval scoops of pâté.

POTATO-LEEK SOUP

6 cups Chicken Stock
2½ pounds white potatoes,
    peeled, cut in eighths

1 yellow onion, sliced
5 ounces unsalted butter
2 leeks, white part only
    Salt and white pepper

1. In saucepan, combine Chicken Stock, potatoes and onion. Cover; bring to a boil and simmer gently for 1 hour.
2. Meanwhile, split leeks lengthwise and rinse well under cold running water. Slice leeks crosswise. Melt 1 stick butter in saucepan, add leeks and cook slowly until limp and golden, about 10 minutes. Do not brown.
3. Drain potatoes and reserve stock. Purée potato-onion mixture and return to stock. Strain potato stock into leeks. Bring to a boil, stirring constantly. Season to taste. Serve topped with a pat of butter if desired.

As with several of the courses in this ambitious menu, the soup may be prepared ahead. Reheat soup in top of double boiler to prevent scorching.

BELGIAN ENDIVE, APPLE, ROQUEFORT AND HAZELNUT SALAD WITH RASPBERRY HAZELNUT VINAIGRETTE

6 ounces hazelnuts
3 Belgian endive (42 leaves)
3 Red Delicious apples, cored,
    each cut in 14 wedges

6 ounces Roquefort cheese,
    crumbled
RASPBERRY HAZELNUT
VINAIGRETTE

1. Roast hazelnuts 10 minutes at 350°; chop coarsely.
2. Separate endive leaves; trim bases to a point. On each chilled plate, arrange 7 endive leaves, petal fashion.

3. Put 1 apple wedge in each leaf. Sprinkle 1 ounce cheese and 1 ounce cooled hazelnuts on each salad.

4. Spoon 4 tablespoons RASPBERRY HAZELNUT VINAIGRETTE over each salad. Salad can be assembled and held 1 hour.

RASPBERRY HAZELNUT VINAIGRETTE

1 cup hazelnut oil	1 tablespoon Dijon mustard
1 cup mild peanut oil	1 teaspoon minced garlic
1 cup raspberry vinegar	

Combine all ingredients and mix well. Refrigerate. Makes 3 cups dressing.

The chef finds many retail peanut oils too strongly flavored. He suggests blending equal parts peanut and safflower oils if a mild oil is not available.

CARAMBOLA CHAMPAGNE SORBET

1 pound ripe carambolas (starfruit)	1 cup sugar
	6 mint spigs
1½ to 1¾ cups Champagne	

1. Dice carambolas; reserve 1 small fruit for garnish.

2. In saucepan, heat sugar in champagne. Boil for 2 minutes. Stir in diced fruit; remove from heat. Purée.

3. Strain mixture through fine sieve. Chill.

4. Process purée in ice cream maker, following manufacturer's directions. Put into covered container; freeze. To serve, let soften in refrigerator 30 minutes. Spoon into chilled stemware; garnish with sliced starfruit and mint.

A 375 milliliter split of champagne may be used. Leftover champagne or a fruity white wine of choice may be substituted.

SAUTÉED BREAST OF CHICKEN
WITH SHIITAKE MUSHROOMS
AND WHOLE GRAIN MUSTARD CREAM SAUCE

12 boneless (6 whole) chicken
   breasts
   Seasoned flour
½ cup Clarified Butter
6 ounces Shiitake mushroom
   caps, sliced
½ cup dry white wine

1½ teaspoons minced shallots
3 cups heavy cream
6 tablespoons whole grain
   mustard, or to taste
6 tablespoons unsalted butter

1. Flatten chicken to ⅜-inch thick. Dust with flour.
2. In large skillet, heat Clarified Butter. Cook chicken breasts gently for 1 minute on each side, until golden but not cooked through. Remove and set aside.
3. Sauté mushrooms in same pan. Add wine and shallots; bring to a boil. Add cream. Bring to a boil and reduce by half, about 10 minutes. Scrape down sides of pan.
4. Stir in mustard. Adjust seasonings.
5. Return chicken to sauce and cook 2 minutes. Just before serving stir in butter and a splash of wine. Serve garnished with tomato and parsley, if desired.

If smaller portions are desired, allow one chicken breast per serving.

TIMBALES OF BROCCOLI, CAULIFLOWER AND CARROT

½ pound carrots, scraped and
   sliced in ½-inch pieces
½ pound cauliflower florettes

½ pound broccoli florettes
1½ cups heavy cream
6 large eggs
   Salt and white pepper

1. In pot with salted water to cover, boil carrots, covered, until very tender, about 20 minutes. Drain.

2. Repeat Step No. 1 with cauliflower and broccoli. Make sure the water is boiling and cook 10 minutes.

3. Purée each vegetable separately in processor or blender. To each, add ½ cup cream. Strain each into a separate bowl. Add 2 beaten eggs to each purée and blend well.

4. Butter 6 large (6 ounce) timbale molds or ramekins and set in a baking pan. Divide broccoli purée in molds up to ⅓ depth. Add 1-inch hot water to pan; cover and steam on very low heat about 10 minutes, just to set surface.

5. Add cauliflower purée; cover and cook until just set. Repeat with carrot purée. Meanwhile, heat oven to 375°. After adding carrots, cover and move water bath with molds to oven for 10 to 15 minutes until timbales are firm.

6. Let cool 5 minutes before turning out of molds. Or, prepare ahead and refrigerate. When ready to serve, reheat 10 to 15 minutes in covered water bath.

Adapting this recipe to pre-cooked or leftover cooked vegetables not only saves time in preparations, but also turns the ordinary into something special. For a decorative touch, place tiny vegetable cutouts in bottom of molds before adding purée. If unstrained purée is used, use more molds.

DAUPHINE POTATOES

1½ *pounds potatoes*
   CHOU PASTE
¼ *cup freshly grated Parmesan
   cheese (1 ounce)*

¼ *teaspoon freshly grated
   nutmeg*
Pinch of white pepper

1. Peel potatoes; cut into eighths and boil until tender. Drain well. Dry in warm oven if too moist. Mash.

2. Combine potatoes, CHOU PASTE, Parmesan cheese, nutmeg and white pepper.

3. Heat oil to 375°. Drop potato mixture by 1-inch scoops or tablespoons into hot oil. Fry for 2 to 3 minutes until golden brown. Drain. Will hold 30 minutes in warm oven.

CHOU PASTE

4 tablespoons unsalted butter
½ cup water
1 teaspoon salt

⅔ cup sifted flour
3 large eggs

1. In saucepan, combine butter, water and salt. Bring to a boil. With wooden spoon, beat in flour, all at once. Reduce heat and cook, stirring, 1 to 2 minutes until dough comes together in a ball. Remove from heat.
2. In mixing bowl, beat eggs into dough one at a time just until absorbed. Use as directed in recipe.

This paste is the basis for cream puff shells and can be spooned onto a baking sheet and baked at 425° until puffed and golden, about 20 to 30 minutes depending on size. Remove from oven, prick shells to vent steam and cool. Spoon or pipe desired filling into shells.

GRAND MARNIER CHOCOLATE TRUFFLE TART

1½ cups heavy cream
2½ tablespoons sugar
7 ounces semisweet chocolate, chopped or grated
3 ounces unsweetened chocolate, chopped or grated

5 egg yolks
3 tablespoons Grand Marnier
   BROWNIE CRUMB CRUST
   Whipped cream, optional

1. In saucepan, bring cream and sugar to a boil. Stir in semisweet and unsweetened chocolates. Remove from heat and stir until smooth.
2. In stainless steel bowl, beat yolks with liqueur. Place bowl over hot water. (Water should be steaming not boiling and should not touch bottom of bowl.) Whisk yolks constantly until fluffy and light yellow.

3. Combine egg yolk and chocolate mixtures, blending well. Pour into prepared BROWNIE CRUMB CRUST. Refrigerate at least 6 hours before serving with garnishes of whipped cream, orange zest or candied peel and a sprig of mint.

BROWNIE CRUMB CRUST

1½ cups CHOCOLATE BROWNIE or cake pieces

6 tablespoons unsalted butter, melted and cooled

In processor or blender, crumb BROWNIE pieces. Blend with cooled butter. Press crumb mixture into bottom and sides of a 9-inch pie pan. Chill until firm.

CHOCOLATE BROWNIE

½ pound (2 sticks) butter
4 ounces unsweetened chocolate
2 cups sugar

3 eggs
1 teaspoon vanilla extract
1 teaspoon salt
1 cup flour

1. In saucepan, melt 1 stick butter and add chocolate.
2. Cream remaining 1 stick butter with sugar. Add eggs, vanilla, salt, flour and melted chocolate/butter.
3. Line a 12"x 17"x 1" jellyroll pan with parchment. Turn batter into pan; bake at 350° for 25 minutes.

The thin Brownie sheet may be cut and used as a dessert base. Or bake 35-40 minutes in a 9"x 12"x 2" pan, until done, for regular brownies.

deux Cheminées

Dinner for Six

Crustacées sur Epinards aux Sauce au Crabe et Whiskey

Batons de Saumon au Nouilles de Safran
aux Sauce Beurre Blanc

Salade de Endive aux Vinaigrette de Printemps

Escalopes de Veau au Sauce Morilles

Glace au Fromage-blanc aux Tuiles

Wines:

With the Shellfish—Chateau de Sancerre, 1984
With the Fish—Chassagne Montrachet, Les Chenevottes, 1983
With the Veal—Volnay-Santenot, Michel Ampeau, 1979

Fritz Blank, Proprietor and Chef

T
he most frequent comment we get," says Fritz Blank, proprietor and chef at Deux Cheminées, "is that dining here is not like dining in a restaurant at all, but rather like dining in someone's home. And we try to convey that feeling. I think 'comfortably classic' is a good description."

Deux Cheminées' menu is eclectically French, based on classic procedures but including a bit of the nouvelle. The regional French influences predominated as well.

Before opening Deux Cheminées, Blank was director of the microbiology department at the Crozer Chester Medical Center. He has degrees in medical technology and dairy science; but cooking was his hobby for years.

"I always loved cooking," he recalls, adding that he learned a lot from his grandmother.

"My German grandmother was an incredible cook. Later I entertained a lot and studied cooking."

Still, cooking was just a hobby until 1979 when Blank was pushed into the business by an associate who found the property and encouraged him to try cooking on a grander scale in his own restaurant. Located on one of Center City's quaint "carriage streets, Deux Cheminées is a renovation of two historically certified townhouses dating back to the early 1800s. It was in this location that Philadelphia's first French restaurant of record, La Coin d'Or, made its home in the late 19th century.

Among the restaurant's more notable decorative features is the striking stained-glass ceiling in the private dining and reception area upstairs. It is a treasure salvaged from the old Taft Hotel in Manhattan. In the main rooms are the two fireplaces, now gas-fueled, from which the restaurant takes its name. Closed for renovations in the fall of 1987, Deux Cheminées is approaching its second decade with a larger, more modern kitchen.

251-253 South Camac Street

CRUSTACES SUR EPINARDS AUX SAUCE
AU CRABE ET WHISKEY

1½ pounds shellfish meats
  (scallops, shrimp, lobster,
  lump crabmeat or a mixture)
6 tablespoons unsalted butter

3 ounces (6 tablespoons)
  Cognac
1 pound spinach
  WHISKEY CRAB SAUCE

1. Sauté shellfish in 4 tablespoons (½ stick) of butter until opaque. Add cognac and flame. Keep warm.
2. Rinse spinach; trim; pat dry and chop. Sauté in remaining 2 tablespoons butter. Divide on warm salad plates.
3. Arrange shellfish on spinach and top with WHISKEY CRAB SAUCE. Garnish as desired with watercress, lemon or lime slices, caviar, a whole cooked crayfish, etc.

Recipe may be served on a bed of braised, julienned endive, with sautéed wild mushrooms, or with segmented sections of grapefruit or tangerine. Or serve in the traditional puffed pastry shells.

WHISKEY CRAB SAUCE

4 tablespoons butter	2 cups FISH STOCK
1 shallot, minced	4 tablespoons thick tomato
1 teaspoon minced garlic	puree
1 pound shredded crabmeat	5 ripe plum tomatoes
1 cup dry white wine or	SHELLFISH BOUQUET
vermouth	GARNI
6 tablespoons Scotch whiskey	1 tablespoon Dijon mustard
6 tablespoons Port	¾ cup heavy cream
	Grapefruit or lemon juice
	Salt and cayenne pepper

1. In heavy 2½-quart saucepan, over medium heat, melt 2 tablespoons butter and lightly sauté shallot, garlic and crabmeat.
2. Add wine, whiskey and Port; flame to burn off alcohol. Add FISH STOCK, tomato purée, tomatoes, SHELLFISH BOUQUET GARNI and mustard. Bring to a boil; reduce to one third.
3. Strain and discard pulp. Add cream; return to a boil and reduce by by one third or to desired consistency.
4. Strain through fine bouillon strainer. Season with a few drops grapefruit juice, salt and cayenne. Whisk in remaining 2 tablespoons butter to finish. Makes about 3 cups.

Sauce is good with seafood, fish or pasta. If you do not plan to serve it at once, the sauce may be thickened only slightly and stablilized with 2 teaspoons Cornstarch Slurry.

FISH STOCK

1 tablespoon corn oil
2 pounds fish heads and bones
2 cups dry white wine or
vermouth
Water

2 carrots, cut up
1 onion, cut up
1 leek, optional
½ lemon
FISH BOUQUET GARNI

1. Heat oil in saucepan over high heat, add fish heads and sauté for 2 minutes. Add 1" water to cover.
2. Add remaining ingredients, bring to a rapid boil, reduce and simmer for 30 minutes.
3. Remove from heat; cool slightly; strain. Discard bones and pulp. Continue reduction to taste. Unused stock can be frozen for up to 3 months. Makes about 1 quart.

Fritz Blank stresses the importance of cooking the bones for fish stock no longer than 30 minutes to avoid bitterness. He recommends use of turbot, sole or swordfish for fish stock. Do not use mackerel or tuna as these species are too oily and have a strong taste.

FISH BOUQUET GARNI

8 sprigs parsley
1 sprig thyme or
½ teaspoon
dried

½ teaspoon fennel seeds
1 bay leaf
6 whole peppercorns

Tie all ingredients together in cheesecloth. Use to flavor fish stocks.

For SHELLFISH BOUQUET GARNI: Proceed as for Fish Bouquet Garni, but omit fennel seeds. Substitute ¼ of a whole nutmeg, crushed.

BATONS DE SAUMON AU NOUILLES DE SAFRAN AUX SAUCE BEURRE BLANC

1 *pound Saffron noodles,*
   cut thin
1½ to 2 *pounds salmon fillets*

Peanut oil
BEURRE BLANC SAUCE

1. Cook noodles until barely tender. Strain; keep warm.
2. Slicing on an angle, cut salmon in medallion-like strips. Space cuts at least 1″ apart on fillet.
3. Brush fish with oil; grill or sauté lightly on both sides, cooking "medium-rare" or still pinkish in center.
4. For each serving, top noodles with 2 or 3 salmon strips and about ⅓ cup BEURRE BLANC SAUCE. Garnish, if desired, with tomato roses or a sprinkling of caviar.

If preferred, this dish may be served with commercial capellini, cooked and tossed with butter and saffron.

BEURRE BLANC SAUCE

1 *cup dry white wine*
¼ *cup white wine vinegar*
⅓ *cup chopped shallots*

2 *cups heavy cream*
½ *pound (2 sticks) unsalted butter, softened*

1. In non-aluminum saucepan, combine wine, vinegar and shallots. Reduce to a glaze on high heat.
2. Deglaze with cream. Bring to a boil; cook 10 minutes. Remove from heat; whisk in butter a few tablespoons at a time. Makes about 2½ cups.

This sauce can be held for 1 hour if kept warm, but cannot be reheated without separation. If desired, flavor the sauce with capers, chervil, dill, lemon, lime, sorrel, thyme or other seasoning, to taste.

SALADE DE ENDIVE AUX VINAIGRETTE DE PRINTEMPS

4 *Belgian endive*   *VINAIGRETTE DE PRINTEMPS*
3 to 4 *ounces watercress*

1. Arrange clean endive leaves and watercress on plates.
2. Drizzle *VINAIGRETTE DE PRINTEMPS* over each.

If desired, crumble a little goat cheese on each salad.

VINAIGRETTE DE PRINTEMPS

3 *scallions, trimmed*   *Pinch of salt, pepper*
½ *cup (½ ounce) basil leaves,*   2 *egg yolks*
   loosely packed   ¼ *cup cider vinegar*
½ *teaspoon sugar*   1½ *cups best quality olive oil*
1 *slice garlic, minced*

1. In blender or processor, combine scallions, basil, sugar, garlic, salt and pepper. Purée, scraping down sides of bowl, until smooth. Transfer to mixing bowl.
2. By hand, whisk in egg yolks and vinegar. Add oil, gradually, beating just to bind ingredients. (Processor or mixer can overbeat, turning the vinaigrette to mayonnaise.) Makes about 2 cups.

If vinaigrette or a similar dressing begins to separate, Blank recommends binding it with 1 teaspoon to 1 tablespoon of egg yolk.

ESCALOPES DE VEAU AU SAUCE MORILLES

*6 veal scallops, 5 ounces each,
about 2 pounds
Flour
Clarified Butter or mild
peanut oil
1 shallot, minced
1 cup Madeira*

*6 ounces morels
2 cups Brown Sauce
4 tablespoons Demi-Glace,
optional
1 tablespoon fresh minced
parsley
¼ pound (1 stick) butter*

1. Dust veal with flour. Sauté in butter. Remove. Keep warm.
2. In same pan, gently sauté shallot. Add Madeira, morels (plus a few tablespoons of liquid if rehydrated), Brown Sauce and Demi-Glace, if available. Reduce by one half.
3. Add parsley. Whisk in butter, by pats, to finish.
4. Serve with reserved veal and, if desired, steamed snowpeas and sautéed cherry tomatoes.

Other wild or cultivated mushrooms like chanterelles or shiitakes may be substituted for morels. Allow 2 or 3 per serving depending on size. Blank suggests avoiding stronger flavored cepes. To reconstitute Dried Mushrooms, see index.

GLACE AU FROMAGE-BLANC

*4⅔ cups heavy cream
1⅓ cups Half & Half
8 egg yolks
1½ cups sugar*

*1 pound fresh goat cheese
TUILES
Shaved chocolate curls*

1. In non-aluminum pot, combine cream and Half & Half. Scald over medium heat by bringing it barely to a boil. Bubbles will appear around edge and a thin skin will form on top.

2. In a processor, blender or bowl, combine egg yolks, sugar and cheese. Add to warm cream. Chill over ice.
3. Process in ice cream maker according manufacturer's directions. Store in freezer. Makes about ½ gallon.
4. Serve in *TUILES*, garnished with chocolate curls.

This unusual ice cream developed by Fritz Blank has a flavor that develops in stages as it dissolves on the tongue. The initial hint of vanilla taste blooms to the flavor of cheese.

TUILES

4 egg whites	*¼ cup finely ground almonds*
1 cup sugar	*¼ pound (1 stick) butter,*
1 cup sifted flour	*melted and cooled*

1. Preheat oven to 375°. Butter a flat cookie sheet or the back of a rimmed baking sheet.
2. With mixer or by hand, beat egg whites and sugar to a glossy, soft meringue. Make sure sugar is dissolved. Gradually sift flour into eggs, beating at low speed, and add remaining ingredients. Mix thoroughly.
3. Spoon by tablespoons onto prepared sheet, spreading batter thin with back of spoon. Tuiles should be 5" to 6" in diameter to form cups; 2" to 3" for cookies. Bake, 1 sheet at a time (2 or 3 large tuiles), at 375° for about 7 minutes, until edges are lightly browned. Remove.
4. Lift gently with a wide spatula and shape warm tuile over inverted glass to form a cup. Repeat with remaining batter. Store tuile cups in airtight container. Makes 20 (thick) to 30 (thin) cups.

The tuiles cool and get crisp very quickly. The first couple may break or crack before you get the timing and technique right. That's why they are made in small batches.

Dinner for Six

Eggplant Roulades

Lobster Ravioli

Grilled Breast of Pheasant with Red Currant Sauce

Fresh Figs Gratin

Wines:

With Roulades—Mastroberardino Lacryma Christi del Vesuvio
With the Ravioli—Gavi di Gavi Broglia
With the Pheasant—Carmignano Ambra, 1983

Joseph DiLullo, Owner
Antonio Schiavone, Restaurant Director
Michael Strumpf, Chef/Centro
Donna Ewanciw, Chef/Fox Chase

J oe DiLullo built his business empire (restaurants and real estate) on a neighborhood pizza shop, Joseph's, in Northeast Philadelphia. In 1979, he opened Ristorante DiLullo next door. Word spread quickly as food lovers from New York to Washington travelled to Fox Chase, a dozen miles from downtown Philadelphia. When DiLullo Centro opened in 1985, it was a second success, a world-class restaurant, in a tough dining town.

DiLullo Centro is a prime example of dinner-as-theater, at the site of the old Locust Street Theatre. The restored marquee and gothic facade are but a prelude to the multimillion dollar interior renovation. A highlight of the sumptuous decor is the muralled wall that wraps around the main dining room. It is a tribute to the Impressionist era and artists like Manet and Van Gogh. Take note, too, of the sculpted bronze table, laden with fresh fruits, vegetables and wines, the private wine cellar/dining room and the glass elevator.

Centro's lush and colorful setting is in sharp contrast to the black and silver chic of Fox Chase, where diners can watch pasta being made in a glass booth off the dining room.

The stages differ but, under the direction of Antonio "Toto" Schiavone, both retain the quality and personal touch of a small restaurant despite glitzy and sybaritic surroundings.

Chef Michael Strumpf supervises the kitchen at DiLullo Centro, producing exciting dishes true to the traditions of Milan, Bologna and Venice. He came to DiLullo's as sous chef in 1985, having been sous chef at Tavern on the Green and at the Hotel Plaza Athénée in Manhattan. Donna Ewanciw, chef at Fox Chase, was sous chef at Tavern on the Green. Both are graduates of the Culinary Institute of America.

1407 Locust Street / Centro
7955 Oxford Avenue / Fox Chase

EGGPLANT ROULADES

1 *firm medium eggplant*
   ANCHOVY-CHEESE BATTER *Oil*
   for frying

CHEESE FILLING
FRESH TOMATO SAUCE
Fresh basil leaves

1. Trim and peel eggplant. Slice lengthwise into 12 flat slices, ⅛" thick. Dip into ANCHOVY-CHEESE BATTER.
2. Heat ¼" oil in skillet, until surface trembles. (Egg will burn in hotter oil.) Fry 4 eggplant slices on both sides to light brown. Repeat with remaining eggplant. Strain or change oil between batches. Drain. Cool.
3. Place 3 to 4 tablespoons CHEESE FILLING at small end of each eggplant slice and roll tightly, being careful not to push out filling. Arrange rolls on lightly oiled sheet pan. (Secure with toothpicks, if necessary.) Bake at 400° for 10 minutes or until light brown.
4. Spoon FRESH TOMATO SAUCE onto warm serving plates. Top with 2 roulades, side by side. Garnish with basil.

Avoid using eggplant slices with a lot of seeds for this dish as they tend to break up and give a bitter flavor. Add eggplant scraps to sauce or reserve for other uses. The roulades may be assembled in advance and finished in the oven just before serving.

ANCHOVY-CHEESE BATTER

2 *anchovy filets*
2 *large eggs*
¼ *cup (1 ounce) grated Parmesan*
   cheese

2 *teaspoons minced basil*
2 to 4 *tablespoons milk*
   Flour

Mash anchovy. Beat in eggs, cheese and basil. Thin slightly with milk. Use as a savory batter for fried foods.

In addition to flavoring mild vegetables, this batter complements veal.

CHEESE FILLING

1 large clove garlic, minced	3 tablespoons freshly grated
4 tablespoons butter	2 romano cheese
2 cups ricotta cheese	1½ egg yolks
½ cup shredded fontina cheese	tablespoons chopped
½ cup shredded mozzarella cheese	oregano
	Freshly ground black
	pepper
	Pinch of salt

1. Sauté garlic lightly in butter. Let cool.
2. In bowl, combine cheeses. Add the garlic and remaining ingredients and mix well. Be careful not to overwork ricotta mixture. (If beaten smooth, ricotta cheese will break down and get runny when baked). Use as directed in recipe. Makes about 3 cups.

FRESH TOMATO SAUCE

3 pounds ripe plum tomatoes	1 teaspoon minced basil or ½
3 tablespoons olive oil	teaspoon dry
1 tablespoon minced shallot	½ teaspoon fresh rosemary or
1 teaspoon minced garlic	¼ teaspoon dry
2 anchovy filets	Salt and pepper
1 teaspoon minced oregano or	
½ teaspoon dry	

1. Peel and seed tomatoes. Purée roughly. Do not blend smooth. You should have at least 4 cups. Set aside.
2. In oil over medium heat, sweat shallot and garlic. Add anchovies, oregano, basil and rosemary; sauté 2 minutes.
3. Add tomato purée; simmer 20 minutes. Season with salt and pepper. Use as directed in recipe. Makes 4 cups.

LOBSTER RAVIOLI

½ recipe LOBSTER FILLING   LOBSTER SAUCE
½ recipe SAFFRON PASTA

1. If not already cut, roll SAFFRON PASTA dough thin, cut into strips 4″ wide.

2. Spoon mounds of LOBSTER FILLING, about 2 teaspoons each, in one row, 1″ apart and ½″ from edge of pasta. Fold pasta strip lengthwise, over filling. Press dough together firmly between fillings and at edges. With pastry cutter, cut between the mounds to make 2″ ravioli squares. Air dry for 2 hours. Cook or refrigerate, well wrapped.

3. Bring a large pot of salted water to a boil and cook ravioli until they rise to the surface. Serve small portions with LOBSTER SAUCE.

The ravioli can be assembled a day ahead. Cooking time will vary with the dryness and thickness of dough. Pasta and filling may be made up to 3 days in advance. Unused portions may be frozen or refrigerated.

LOBSTER FILLING

Tails and claws of 4 lobsters,
see LOBSTER STOCK
2 tablespoons butter
4 shallots, chopped fine
¾ cup brandy
2 teaspoons chopped tarragon

1½ teaspoons chopped parsley
3 cups heavy cream
Salt and freshly ground
black pepper
¼ teaspoon cayenne pepper
1½ to 2 cups fresh white bread
crumbs, crusts removed

1. Split tails, crack claws and steam 4 to 5 minutes in pot with ½" water. Drain. Cool; remove and chop meat.

2. In skillet, sauté shallots in butter. Add lobster meat; stir 1 minute on high heat. Add brandy; reduce by one third. Add cream, reduce until thick and remove from heat.

3. Add salt, pepper and cayenne. Cool over ice to room temperature. Add crumbs to absorb some, but not all moisture. (Add crumbs after mixture cools because sauce tightens a bit naturally). Makes enough for 6 entrée or 12 appetizer portions.

Add the liquid from steamed lobster to LOBSTER STOCK. *Extra filling can be used to stuff fish or toss with pasta.*

LOBSTER STOCK

4 lobsters, 1½ to 2 pounds each
¼ cup olive oil
½ cup brandy
1 large onion, diced
1 carrot, diced
2 ribs celery, diced

1 leek, diced
2 shallots, chopped
1 large clove garlic, minced
3 cups dry white wine
1 HERB SACHET
4 cups crushed plum
tomatoes

1. Kill lobsters by cutting off tail where it joins the body, or split lengthwise.
2. Remove heads and legs. Split heads; discard sand sacs. Chop heads and legs in smaller pieces. (Reserve tail and claw meat for *LOBSTER FILLING*. Save any roe and tomalley for other uses.)
3. In saucepan with olive oil, sauté lobster heads and legs until shells are bright red. Add brandy and cook off.
4. Add onions, carrot, celery, leek, shallots and garlic; sauté. Add wine and *HERB SACKET*; reduce by one half.
5. Add tomatoes and cook 10 minutes more.
6. Add water to bring stock 3" over shells. Bring to a boil and simmer 40 minutes. Skim surface frequently. At desired flavor strength, remove *HERB SACHET*. Strain stock. Remove and discard the hardest shells. Pass shells and vegetables through a food mill or processor. Strain through fine meshed sieve. Freeze in cups for use in sauce. Makes 2 to 2½ quarts.

Fresh tomatoes are preferable in this dish, says chef Ewanciw, because tomato paste gives it a bitter flavor.

HERB SACHET

To make Herb Sachet: Tie together in cheesecloth bag, 5 sprigs parsley, 4 sprigs thyme, 1 sprig tarragon, 1 bay leaf and 1 tablespoon black peppercorns. Use as seasoning.

SAFFRON PASTA

1 teaspoon saffron threads	1 teaspoon oil
2 tablespoons warm water	½ teaspoon salt
3 large eggs	2¼ to 2½ cups Durum wheat flour

1. Crumble saffron in water; let stand 5 minutes.
2. Beat together eggs, oil, salt and saffron water.
3. In bowl or processor, combine 2¼ cups flour with eggs until it forms a soft ball. Add more flour or water as needed. Knead until satiny and elastic. Let rest 30 minutes.
4. Roll by hand or machine, cutting to desired size. Or, refrigerate or freeze, well wrapped, for later use. Makes 1 pound, enough for 6 entrée or 12 appetizer portions.

If all-purpose flour is substituted for the harder (higher gluten) Durum, less additional water will be needed.

LOBSTER SAUCE

1 cup LOBSTER STOCK	½ pound (2 sticks) unsalted
1 cup heavy cream	butter

1. Shortly before serving, over high heat, reduce LOBSTER STOCK by one half. Add cream and reduce by one half again.
2. Reduce heat to low. Whisk in butter, by pats. Be careful sauce neither overheats nor cools. Add salt and pepper to taste. Keep warm until ready to serve. Makes 2 to 2½ cups.

GRILLED BREAST OF PHEASANT WITH RED CURRANT SAUCE

3 *pheasants, 1½ to 2 pounds*   JUNIPER MARINADE
each, split, breast bones   RED CURRANT SAUCE
removed, wings and legs
intact, bones reserved

1. In baking pan, 3 or 4 days ahead, coat pheasant with JUNIPER MARINADE. Refrigerate, turning twice daily.
2. At serving time, grill 5 to 8 minutes to imprint grill pattern, and finish in a 375° oven for 15 to 20 minutes. Or, roast at 375° for 25 minutes for medium moist meat.
3. Serve with RED CURRANT SAUCE.

This recipe is also delicious with duck.

JUNIPER MARINADE

2 *cups olive oil*   1 *tablespoon cracked black*
¼ *cup Port*   *peppercorns*
1 *shallot, minced*   1½ *teaspoons chopped thyme*
1½ *tablespoons cracked juniper*
berries

Combine all ingredients in bowl. Use to marinate fowl or meat. Makes about 2½ cups.

RED CURRANT SAUCE

1 tablespoon unsalted butter	1 teaspoon peppercorns
2 tablespoons chopped onion	½ cup red currant purée
1 clove garlic	¾ cup dry vermouth
3 sprigs parsley	2¼ cups rich PHEASANT
1 sprig thyme	STOCK
1 bay leaf	Salt and pepper

1. Melt butter in saucepan; sauté chopped onion 1 minute. Add garlic, parsley, thyme, bay and peppercorns. Add currant purée and simmer until reduced and syrupy, about 5 minutes.
2. Add vermouth and reduce by one-half.
3. Add PHEASANT STOCK; reduce to consistency of light cream. Strain. Adjust seasoning. Serve with pheasant.

Fresh red currants are in season in June and July. Frozen red currant purée is available through some specialty food sources. As an alternative, substitute raspberries for red currants and add ¼ cup white vinegar. Or, eliminate fruit purée, and substitute Port for the vermouth.

PHEASANT STOCK

Reserved bones of 3 pheasants	1 teaspoon dried thyme
1 large onion, cut up	½ teaspoon dried rosemary
1 carrot, cut up	1 bay leaf
2 ribs celery, cut up	1 teaspoon cracked juniper
1 small leek, cut up	berries
¼ cup Port	1 teaspoon whole black
4 sprigs parsley	peppercorns
1 clove garlic	

1. Roast pheasant bones in 400° oven until light brown. Transfer to stock pot; add at least 10 cups water to cover by 2". Bring to a boil; simmer 1 hour, skimming frequently.

2. Meanwhile, sauté onion, carrot, celery and leek in pheasant drippings in roasting pan until translucent. When bones have simmered 1 hour, add vegetables. Deglaze roasting pan with Port. Add to stockpot. In cheesecloth, tie together parsley, garlic, thyme, rosemary, bay, juniper and peppercorns. Add to stockpot. Simmer 3 hours more. Strain.

3. Continue reduction to about 6 cups rich stock. Use or freeze.

FRESH FIGS GRATIN

10 fresh figs
  6 tablespoons Cointreau

1 cup heavy cream
½ cup PASTRY CREAM

1. Preheat oven to 500°.

2. Cut figs in ¼″ slices. Divide among 6 gratin dishes. Splash 1 tablespoon Cointreau on each portion.

2. Whip cream just until it begins to mound.

3. Fold whipped cream into PASTRY CREAM. Spoon over figs to cover. Brown lightly in 500° oven, 3 to 4 minutes.

PASTRY CREAM

1¾ cups milk
  ⅛ cup sugar

1 egg plus 1 yolk, beaten
1 teaspoon butter
⅛ teaspoon vanilla extract

1. In saucepan, bring milk and sugar to a simmer.

2. Add eggs to hot milk, whisking briskly. Eggs will cook in milk if not done quickly; you may whip a small amount of hot milk into the eggs first to equalize their temperature with the milk. Beat over medium-low heat 2 to 3 minutes until thickened. Stir in butteer and vanilla. Makes about 2 cups.

Dinner for Six

Broiled Oysters
with Bacon, Parmesan and Horseradish

Seafood Gazpacho

Warm Spinach, Arugula and Basil Salad
with Pine Nuts, Roasted Peppers and Goat Cheese

Grilled Tuna with Tomato, Eggplant and Fennel Ragout
and Roasted Garlic Butter

Peach-Blueberry Streusel Pie

Wines:

With the Oysters and Gazpacho—Vino Verde
With the Tuna—Gavi di Gavi, Broglia

Paul & Becky Roller, Owners
Richard Roller, General Manager
Beth Cooper, Chef
Melanie Carson Melle, Pastry Chef

Paul and Becky Roller met and married in 1979 while working within the 16th Street Bar and Grill/Commissary restaurant group in town.

"We discussed Paul's opening his own restaurant on our first date, never dreaming that I would be involved in it, too," Becky recalls.

"Our feeling always was that we would fulfill a need for a casual place for working people, the kind of place where we would want to go every week, not just on special occasions."

The couple brought that concept home to Paul's Chestnut Hill neighborhood, opening Roller's Cafe in 1982. In 1984, they added Roller's Market (for gourmet provisions and take-out). The Flying Fish was opened a year later in a more formal setting but with comparable prices.

Although dressed in contemporary decor, the restaurant conveys the essense of a classic fish house right down to the oyster crackers and horseradish at each table. Some of the same recipes turn up on the menus of both restaurants, but seafoods predominate at Flying Fish.

"We try to keep our food interesting without being precious," this working chef says of his ever evolving food repertoire. "Our whole menu is designed for preparation in a small kitchen, so our recipes are easy to make at home."

But then translating restaurant recipes for home cooks is second nature for Becky, who co-authored and illustrated The Frog/Commissary Cookbook. The important extras in the Roller's homestyle approach are an unstinting devotion to the best and freshest ingredients, unerring taste buds and an abundance of imagination.

8142 Germantown Avenue

BROILED OYSTERS WITH BACON, PARMESAN
AND HORSERADISH

24 *medium oysters, Long Island*
    or Maryland, in shells
 6 *strips of bacon*
 4 *tablespoons horseradish*
 2 *tablespoons lemon juice*

12 *drops hot pepper sauce*
½ *cup (2 ounces) grated*
    Parmesan cheese
 1 *lemon, cut in 6 wedges*

1. Shuck oysters, discarding top shells. Loosen oyster in bottom shell. Arrange on a broiler tray.
2. Preheat broiler.
3. Cut bacon in pieces 1½-inch long; blanch for 1½ to 2 minutes in boiling water. Drain. Reserve.
4. In small bowl, combine horseradish, lemon juice and hot pepper sauce; blend well.
5. Top each oyster with ¾ teaspoon of horseradish mixture, spreading lightly. Place a piece of blanched bacon on each oyster. Sprinkle 1 teaspoon of cheese over each oyster. Broil, about 6 inches from heat source, for 5 minutes or until oysters begin to curl and bacon browns. Garnish with lemon wedges and chopped parsley or watercress, if desired.

SEAFOOD GAZPACHO

18 mussels (about 1½ pounds)
1½ cups dry white wine
1 bay leaf
6 large shrimp, peeled
2 small carrots, finely chopped
1 medium cucumber, peeled,
seeded and chopped
1 small green pepper, seeded
and chopped
5 scallions, finely chopped
2 ribs celery, without leaves,
finely chopped

1 can (46 ounces) tomato juice
2 tablespoons lemon juice
2 tablespoons red wine vinegar
2 tablespoons olive oil
1 teaspoon minced garlic (2 or 3
cloves)
6 drops hot pepper sauce
½ teaspoon salt
½ teaspoon pepper
½ cup lump crabmeat

1. In advance, scrub and debeard mussels. Steam in wine with bay until shells open. Remove; shell. Reserve.

2. Add shrimp; cook 3 minutes or until opaque. Remove and chop. Reserve. Strain mussel/wine broth.

3. Meanwhile, in pot or large pitcher, combine tomato juice, carrots, cucumber, green pepper, celery and scallions. Reserve 1 tablespoon scallions for garnish.

4. Stir in lemon juice, vinegar, oil, garlic, hot pepper sauce, salt and pepper. Add wine broth. Chill for 3 hours or more to meld flavors. Adjust seasonings.

5. Before serving, add reserved mussels and shrimp. When served, garnish each portion with a generous tablespoon of lump crabmeat and ½ teaspoon reserved scallion.

Because tomato juice is a key ingredient in this recipe, Paul emphasizes the importance of using a thick, rich product. This soup is best made a day ahead.

WARM SPINACH, ARUGULA AND BASIL SALAD WITH PINE NUTS, ROASTED PEPPERS AND GOAT CHEESE

1 roasted red bell pepper
⅓ cup toasted pine nuts
1 pound fresh spinach, torn
1 bunch arugula, 4 to 6 ounces
1 bunch basil, about 18 large leaves

½ cup extra-virgin olive oil
¼ cup Balsamic vinegar
¼ teaspoon salt
¼ teaspoon pepper
¼ pound fresh goat cheese

1. To roast pepper: Char peppers evenly over an open flame or broil or bake at 475°-500° for 20 minutes or until blistered and black. Let cool. Peel and seed. Cut into thin strips. If not used same day, store covered with olive oil.
2. To toast pine nuts: Sauté nuts in a little oil until lightly browned; or spread in baking pan and bake at 475° for 5 minutes or until lightly browned, stirring occasionally.
3. Wash spinach, arugula and basil; pat dry.
4. In sauté pan, heat oil and vinegar very hot, until vinegar starts to boil. Add pinenuts, salt and pepper.
5. Toss greens and hot dressing in metal bowl. Hold bowl over heat for about 30 seconds to slightly wilt greens.
6. Divide salad on plates. Garnish with roasted peppers and crumbled goat cheese, about 1 tablespoon for each portion.

Fresh goat cheese is now available to area restaurants and food shops thanks to another former Commissary chef, Douglass Newbold, and her flock of Nubian goats.

GRILLED TUNA WITH TOMATO, EGGPLANT AND FENNEL RAGOUT AND ROASTED GARLIC BUTTER

6 *tuna steaks, ½ inch thick,*
  about 6 ounces each
Olive oil
Salt and fresh ground pepper

Lemon juice
TOMATO, EGGPLANT AND
FENNEL RAGOUT
ROASTED GARLIC BUTTER

1. Brush tuna with oil. Sprinkle with salt, pepper and lemon juice. Grill 2 to 3 minutes on each side, until just pink in the center.*
2. Serve tuna on a bed of *TOMATO, EGGPLANT AND FENNEL RAGOUT.* Top with a dollop of *ROASTED GARLIC BUTTER.*

* *Tuna should be cooked just slightly rare because it dries out more quickly than other fish. Also, residual heat continues the cooking process after removing the fish from the pan.*

TOMATO, EGGPLANT AND FENNEL RAGOUT

½ *large Spanish onion, sliced*
½ *medium eggplant, sliced*
  lengthwise
1 *fennel bulb, sliced lengthwise*
  Olive oil
  Salt and pepper

1 *pound plum tomatoes,*
  coarsely chopped
1 *tablespoon lemon juice*
1 *tablespoon chopped, mixed,*
  fresh herbs (basil, oregano,
  parsley)

1. Brush onion, eggplant and fennel slices with oil. Sprinkle with salt and pepper. Grill or sauté vegetables a few minutes until tender-crisp. Cut in 1½-inch pieces.
2. In large skillet, sauté tomatoes with 4 tablespoons oil until soft. Add lemon juice, herbs and ½ teaspoon each salt and pepper. Add vegetables. Makes about 6 cups.

This ragout also is a good sauce for pastas. The integrity of the vegetables is maintained.

FLYING FISH

ROASTED GARLIC BUTTER

1 large head garlic
1 teaspoon olive oil
1 teaspoon chopped parsley

½ teaspoon lemon juice
½ pound (1 stick) unsalted
  butter, softened
  Salt and pepper

1. Break garlic head into cloves, leaving skin on. Smash cloves slightly with mallet or cleaver. Toss garlic with oil. Bake at 375° for 15 minutes or until soft. Peel and purée.
2. To garlic purée, add parsley, lemon juice and butter; blend well. Add salt and pepper, to taste. Chill until ready to use. Or, wrap airtight and freeze.

PEACH-BLUEBERRY STREUSEL PIE

1-2-3 COOKIE CRUST DOUGH,
½ recipe
2 *pounds fresh peaches*
2 *pints fresh blueberries*
4 *ounces cream cheese*

1 *cup sour cream*
1 *cup sugar*
¼ *cup flour*
2 *teaspoons vanilla extract*
1 *large egg*
STREUSEL TOPPING

1. On lightly floured surface, roll dough about ¼-inch thick to fit a 10-inch fluted tart pan, 2 inches deep, with removeable bottom. Butter sides of pan. Press dough into flutes.
2. Preheat oven to 450°.
3. Halve, pit and peel peaches. Score outer surface with diagonal crosshatch cuts, ¼-inch deep. Arrange peaches, cut side down, in tart shell. Chop and add any extra peach halves. Stem blueberries and add to peaches in tart shell.
4. In mixing bowl, beat cream cheese with sour cream, sugar, flour, vanilla and egg until smooth. Pour into tart. Bake at 450° for 10 minutes. Reduce heat to 350° and bake 35 minutes more. Meanwhile, prepare STREUSEL TOPPING.
5. Sprinkle STREUSEL TOPPING over pie. Bake 10-15 minutes more. Let cool completely. Remove pan rim. Serve.

The fruit filling of this pie may be varied with the seasons. Using alternative fresh fruits, says Paul, is preferable to a canned substitute.

1-2-3 COOKIE CRUST DOUGH

1 *pound unsalted butter,*　　　2 *extra large egg yolks*
 softened　　　　　　　　　　3 *cups all-purpose flour*
1 *cup sugar*

1. In mixing bowl, cream butter and sugar. Beat in yolks. Work in flour, 1 cup at a time, to form soft dough.
2. Chill before using. Or divide, wrap and freeze. Makes enough for 2 large, deep dish (or 3 medium) tarts.

   Extra dough also may be used for cookies. Roll; slice and bake at 350° for 7-9 minutes, until golden.

STREUSEL TOPPING

1½ *cups walnuts (6 ounces)*　　4 *tablespoons (½ stick) butter,*
 ⅓ *cup brown sugar*　　　　　　 *cut up*
 ⅓ *cup white sugar*　　　　　　1 *tablespoon cinnamon*
 ½ *cup flour*

1. In blender or processor, combine walnuts, brown and white sugars, flour, butter and cinnamon. Chop in short pulses until walnuts are in small pieces.
2. Sprinkle over pie for last 10-15 minutes of baking.

Dinner for Four

Oyster Mushroom Cream Soup

Endive Salad with Sautéed American Fresh Foie Gras

Poached Escalope of Salmon with Olive Oil and Tomato

Veal Medallions in Shallot Sauce

Lost Bread with Apple and Caramel Sauce

Wines:

With the Foie Gras—Vouvray, 1979, Prince Poniatowsky
With the Salmon—Chardonnay, 1983, Spring Mountain
With the Veal—Chianti Classico Riserva, 1979, Berardenga

Albert Farkas, Manager
Jean-Marie Lacroix, Executive Chef
Bruce Lim, Fountain Chef

Consistently rated among Philadelphia's finest restaurants, The Fountain at the world-class Four Seasons Hotel is as popular with area residents as with tourists. The Fountain has achieved that rare combination of intimacy within hotel grandeur. Large windows face out on two favored Philadelphia views—Logan Square and The Benjamin Franklin Parkway. The blend of both sophistication and comfort found in the columned restaurant and the neighboring Swann Lounge make this an enjoyable stop for diners who demand service and surroundings as impressive as the food. Here snackers can enjoy finger sandwiches and scones at afternoon tea; hors d'oeuvres during the cocktails hours; or a late night dessert and flaming coffee served with a piano accompaniment. Between the dining room and the lounge, the Swann Cafe offers a lighter, transitional menu throughout the day.

Along with its international menu, The Fountain was among the first restaurants in the area to add a low-calorie spa-style menu, one offered not just to participants in the hotel's weekend spa program but to the public as well. Some of those same health-conscious cooking techniques have been incorporated into The Fountain's regular menu without compromising on taste. And there has developed a larger Alternative Cuisine Menu for diners concerned with their intake of calories, cholesterol and sodium.

Credit for the hotel's fine food operation goes to Executive Chef Jean-Marie Lacroix. Trained at Thonon Les Bains on Lake Geneva, Lacroix was Executive Chef at The Four Seasons in Montreal before coming to Philadelphia. In earlier posts, he was Chef at the Royal Lancaster Hotel in London and the Turnberry and Gleneagles Hotels in Scotland.

Born in Singapore, raised and trained in France, Chef Bruce Lim brings his own special personality and creativity to The Fountain menu. He has worked at Le Pavillon and Jean-Louis in Washington, D.C., and at Montrachet in New York.

One Logan Square

OYSTER MUSHROOM CREAM SOUP

6 to 8 ounces oyster mushrooms
2 shallots, minced
1 clove garlic, minced
1 tablespoon unsalted butter

2 cups VEGETABLE CONSOMME
or Chicken Broth
2 cups heavy cream
Salt and white pepper

1. In saucepan, over low heat, cook mushrooms, shallots and garlic with butter for 4 minutes. Add VEGETABLE CONSOMME and cream. Simmer gently for 10 minutes.
2. Transfer, in batches, to blender and purée. Serve.

VEGETABLE CONSOMME

1½ quarts water
1 piece (2 inches) carrot, diced
1 piece (2 inches) celery, diced

1 scallion, chopped
½ small turnip, diced
1 clove garlic, chopped
10 whole peppercorns

1. In 2-quart saucepan, combine water, carrot, celery, scallion, turnip, garlic and peppercorns. Bring to a boil; let simmer on moderate-low heat for 20 minutes.
2. Strain broth. Freeze unused broth in 1 cup containers. Makes about 1 quart.

ENDIVE SALAD WITH SAUTÉED AMERICAN FOIE GRAS

4 slices fresh foie gras, 1-inch
thick, about 4 ounces each
Salt and pepper
3 tablespoons walnut oil

1 tablespoon red wine vinegar
4 whole Belgian endives

1. Heat a dry, non-stick skillet very hot. Sear foie gras for 2 minutes on each side. Salt and pepper, to taste.
2. In bowl, combine oil and vinegar. Cut endives in 2-inch pieces and toss with dressing. Divide on plates and top with warm foie gras.

POACHED ESCALOPE OF SALMON
WITH OLIVE OIL AND TOMATO

4 pieces salmon fillet, 6 ounces
each (1½ pounds)
2 teaspoons extra-virgin olive
oil
2 teaspoons Vegetable Consomme or Chicken Broth

2 ripe tomatoes, diced, with
juice
1 clove garlic, chopped
10 leaves fresh basil, chopped
2 tablespoons butter

1. Put salmon in sauté pan with oil, consomme, tomato and garlic. Bring to a simmer. Cook, over low heat, for about 3 minutes on each side for fish ½-inch to ¾-inch thick.
2. Transfer salmon to warm serving plates; keep warm.
3. Add basil and butter to sauce; increase heat and whisk together to finish. Serve over poached salmon.

SAUTÉED VEAL MEDALLIONS WITH SHALLOT SAUCE

2 cups Vegetable Consomme
8 veal medallions, ¼ inch thick,
   3 ounces each (1½ pounds)
6 tablespoons unsalted butter

8 shallots, minced
2 tablespoons Veal Stock or beef
   stock
Parsley for garnish

1. In advance, in saucepan over medium-high heat, bring Vegetable Consomme to boiling and reduce by a third, about 20 minutes. Set aside.
2. In skillet, over medium heat, sauté veal in 2 tablespoons of butter for 1 minute on each side. Add salt and pepper, to taste. Transfer to warm platter; keep warm.
3. Add 2 tablespoons butter to skillet and sauté the shallots for 2 minutes. Add Veal Stock and reserved reduction of Vegetable Consomme. Bring to boiling. Let simmer gently for 10 minutes.
4. Meanwhile, heat oven to 350°. Divide 1 tablespoon butter over veal medallions; bake at 350° about 4 minutes.
5. Transfer sauce to blender and purée. Whisk in remaining 1 tablespoon butter. Serve with veal. Garnish with parsley. If desired, accompany with sautéed snowpeas.

To keep foods warm, set oven to temperature low enough that no further cooking will take place. For meat, this would be 150° for medium, or 140° for rare.

LOST BREAD WITH APPLE AND CARAMEL SAUCE

2 *Granny Smith apples, peeled*
and cored
5 *tablespoons butter*
1 *tablespoons sugar*
½ *cup heavy cream*

2 *egg yolks*
2 *tablespoons superfine sugar*
4 *slices French bread, 1" thick*
   CARAMEL SAUCE

1. Cut each apple into 6 wedges. In sauté pan, over medium heat, melt 3 tablespoons butter and sugar. Add apple wedges and cook for 2 minutes until golden brown. Remove and keep warm.

2. In a bowl, beat together heavy cream, egg yolks and superfine sugar. Dip bread in cream mixture to soak, about 2 minutes.

3. In a skillet, over medium heat, melt the remaining 2 tablespoons of butter. Fry soaked bread slices for 2 to 3 minutes, until golden brown.

4. Place one toast slice on each dessert plate. Spoon 3 apple wedges on top of each and pour *CARAMEL SAUCE* around toast. If desired, use a teaspoon of cream to make a little design on top of the caramel sauce, by cutting or swirling.

It is better to use two- or three-day-old bread for this fancy French toast. To avoid having the Caramel Sauce be too sweet, make sure the sugar is cooked until it is dark brown.

CARAMEL SAUCE

1 *cup sugar*   1 *cup heavy cream*

In a saucepan over medium heat, melt the sugar and cook, stirring, for about 2 minutes until sugar is caramelized and dark brown. Whisk the cream into the caramel. Bring to a boil and let cook for 1 minute. Set aside to cool. Makes about 1 cup.

Le
Bec - Fin

Dinner for Four

Salade de Crabe

Rouget au Beurre Rouge ala Moelle

Veau au Citron

Gratin Dauphinois

Sorbet au Cassis

Gâteau au Chocolat Le Bec-Fin

Wines:

With the Crab—Tokay d'Alsace "Les Murailles" 1975
With Fish—Puligny Montrachet "Les Combettes" Leflave 1980
With the Veal—Beune Greves Duchet 1964
With the Cake—Louis Roederer Carte Blanche

Georges Perrier, Proprietor and Chef

97

LE BEC-FIN

Acclaimed internationally as one of America's finest restaurants, Le Bec-Fin, and its equally acclaimed chef/owner Georges Perrier, offer the ultimate in dining elegance and sophisticated French cooking.

In a setting that rivals Versailles, patrons dine regally, lingering over a five-course, prix fixe (as of this writing $76 per person) dinner with embellishments at every pause in the unobtrusively attentive service. That service includes Limoges china and Christofle silver, and is presented in a room appointed with three huge crystal chandeliers, lavish floral arrangements, chestnut balloon-back chairs and silk damask wall coverings.

Master Chef Perrier opened his restaurant in 1970, choosing as its name the French idiom for "the good taste." And indeed the "fine nose" and sharp senses of the chef monitor the flavor of every sauce, the quality of every ingredient and the artistry of every garnish that comes out of the kitchen.

Building on his training at the renowned L'osteau Baumaniere in Provence and La Pyramide in Vienne, Perrier came to America in 1967 as chef at the old La Panetiére.

Le Bec-Fin began in the small, Spruce Street townhouse that had been La Panetiére. It moved to its present location in 1983. Recognized as a world-class saucier, Perrier has been inducted into the elite order of French master chefs, Maîtres Cuisiniers de France and the equally prestigious Academie Culinaire de France.

While maintaining the integrity of classic style, the chef is continually creating new dishes that reflect his own enthusiasm and excitement about food. But the roguish Frenchman resists categorization.

"This is Georges Perrier's cooking," he says with a hint of mischief in his voice. "It's one of a kind."

1523 Walnut Street

Le Bec-Fin

SALADE DE CRABE

1 pound lump crabmeat
1 tablespoon salad oil
1 teaspoon red wine vinegar
12 leaves Belgian endive

4 ounces mixed greens (mache,
    radicchio, Boston lettuce)
GREEN PEPPER MAYONNAISE
BALSAMIC VINAIGRETTE

1. Pick over crabmeat and discard shells.
2. Heat oil in non-stick skillet. Sauté crab to light golden color; deglaze pan with wine vinegar. Set aside.
3. Fill endive leaves with GREEN PEPPER MAYONNAISE. Arrange 3 leaves on each plate.
4. Toss greens with BALSAMIC VINAIGRETTE. Divide on plates. Divide reserved crab over greens.

If desired, substitute crab cakes for lump crabmeat on salad.

GREEN PEPPER MAYONNAISE

1 green pepper, seeded   5 tablespoons MAYONNAISE

Roast pepper at 450° until skin is charred; peel. Puree pepper flesh, blending with MAYONNAISE. Makes ½ cup.

MAYONNAISE

1 large egg
1 tablespoon vinegar or lemon
  juice
⅛ teaspoon prepared mustard
  or a pinch of dry

Pinch of salt and
white pepper
⅔ cup oil

1. In blender or with whisk in a warm bowl, whip egg.
2. Beat in vinegar, mustard, salt and pepper.
3. Starting with drops and slowly increasing to a thin stream, whip oil into the egg base. Makes about ¾ cup.

Perrier uses whole eggs, rather than yolks only, because "it makes a lighter mayonnaise."

BALSAMIC VINAIGRETTE

1 teaspoon prepared mustard
¼ cup balsamic vinegar
½ cup walnut oil

½ teaspoon chives
½ teaspoon chervil

Combine all ingredients ina blender. Blend well, Makes ¾ cup.

ROUGET AU BEURRE ROUGE A LA MOELLE

12 pieces bone marrow (most
   butchers carry it)
 2 pounds Florida red snapper
   or French red mullet fillets
   (4 pieces, 8 ounces each)

1 tablespoon oil
  Salt and white pepper
  BEURRE ROUGE
8 whole scallions

1. Poach bone marrow in boiling water, 2 to 3 minutes. Strain. Set aside; keep warm.
2. In non-stick skillet, sauté fish fillets in oil.
3. In another pan, sauté whole scallions.
4. Place fish on warmed plates, a scallion on each side. Top with 3 pieces bone marrow; surround with sauce.

BEURRE ROUGE

6½ cups (1½ liters) Zinfandel
2 shallots, chopped
2 sprigs thyme
1 teaspoon sugar
3 tablespoons FISH STOCK
1 to 2 ounces fresh fish meat, shredded

2 scallions, green only, chopped
1 pound (4 sticks) plus tablespoon butter
2 tablespoons oil

1. In heavy saucepan, bring wine, shallots and thyme to a boil. With great care, flame wine to burn off alcohol. It takes a few minutes and flames reach well above the pot. (Keep a lid handy to cover and extinguish if necessary.)
2. Add sugar, FISH STOCK, and fish. Bring to a boil and reduce to one half, about 20 to 30 minutes.
3. Meanwhile, sauté scallions in 1 tablespoon butter until they loose color. Add to sauce. Add 1 pound butter, in pieces and reduce by one half again.
4. Pass sauce through chinois or fine mesh strainer. Discard vegetable/fish pulp. Keep warm for serving, up to 2 hours. Keep excess refrigerated. Makes about 3 cups.

The secret to this sauce, says Perrier, is to cook it slowly and with care. Allow 1 to 1½ hours minimum.

FISH STOCK

10 pounds clean fish bones	3 bay leaves
2 carrots, chopped	1 teaspoon black peppercorns
2 medium onions, chopped	1 bunch parsley stems (leaves
4 ribs celery, cut up	reserved for other uses)
1 tablespoon thyme	1 gallon water

Place all ingredients in a stock pot and bring to a boil. Skim foam and simmer 15 minutes. Strain. Refrigerate up to 3 days or freeze.

Perrier suggests you use sole, monkfish, flounder or turbot bones for the stock. No gills or innards or bones from oily fish should be used.

VEAU AU CITRON

1 pound loin of veal (8 medallions, 2 ounces each)	Juice of 2 lemons (½ cup)
2 tablespoons flour	1 teaspoon chives
1 tablespoon oil	1 teaspoon chervil
2 tablespoons dry vermouth	1 cup Chicken Stock
	½ teaspoon butter

1. Dredge veal in flour, tapping to remove excess.
2. Heat oil in skillet and brown veal, 1 to 2 minutes on each side. Remove; set aside. Keep warm.
3. Deglaze pan with vermouth. Add lemon juice, chives, chervil and Chicken Stock. Bring to a boil; reduce by one third, 5 minutes.
4. Return veal to pan with sauce, and simmer 1 minute. Stir in butter to finish. Serve accompanied, if desired, by a steamed or sautéed green vegetable such as spinach, snowpeas, or string beans.

GRATIN DAUPHINOIS

1 clove garlic, peeled, halved
1 tablespoon butter
6 medium baking potatoes, peeled

Salt and white pepper
1 cup heavy cream
½ cup whole milk

1. Rub bottom and sides of a 1½-quart baking dish with garlic, then with butter.
2. Slice potatoes ⅛" or thinner; arrange in dish in overlapped layers. Cover with mixture of cream and milk.
3. Set dish in a pan of hot water and bake at 350°, 2 to 2½ hours.

SORBET AU CASSIS

6 cups black currant juice (strained purée)
½ cup Simple Syrup

¼ cup (2 ounces) water
Juice of ½ lemon (2 tablespoons)

Combine all ingredients in ice cream or gelato maker. Follow manufacturer's directions on the machine. Makes about 1½ quarts.

Black currants are available, bottled, at some gourmet food shops. A fruit liqueur may be substituted for the water, if desired. Orange or other citrus juices may be used in place of lemon.

GÂTEAU AU CHOCOLAT LE BEC-FIN

½ cup sifted all-purpose flour
2 tablespoons cocoa powder
½ teaspoon baking powder
4 large eggs, separated

5 tablespoons sugar
RUM SYRUP
BUTTERCREAM FROSTING
Chocolate shavings, curls or
jimmies for decoration

1. Sift together flour, cocoa and baking powder.
2. Beat egg whites to soft peaks. Add 1 tablespoon of sugar; beat 1 minute more. Set aside.
3. Preheat oven to 325°. Butter and flour a 9″ layer pan.
4. In mixer bowl set over hot (not boiling) water, whip yolks and remaining ¼ cup sugar; heat to 150° or hot to the touch, just steaming. Whip until egg cream forms ribbons off the whisk.
5. Sift flour over egg cream, folding in gently. Fold reserved egg whites into batter. Turn into prepared pan.
6. Bake at 325°, 30 minutes or until cake tests done.
7. Turn onto rack and cool completely before slicing horizontally into 2 or 3 thin layers, as desired.
8. To assemble, place bottom layer of cake on serving plate. Drizzle lightly with *RUM SYRUP*; spread with ⅓ to ½ *BUTTERCREAM FROSTING*, depending on number of cake layers. Repeat with remaining cake layer or layers, syrup and frosting. Decorate as desired. Refrigerate

The thickness of frosting here is roughly equal to the thickness of the cake itself. It is a rich dessert. "Jimmies" is Philadelpia jargon for "sprinkles."

RUM SYRUP

½ cup sugar   1 to 2 ounces rum
½ cup boiling water

Make a *SIMPLE SYRUP* by dissolving sugar in boiling water. Remove from heat; cool and add rum, to taste.

BUTTERCREAM FROSTING

4 large eggs   7 ounces (1¾ sticks) unsalted
¾ cup sugar   butter, softened
8 ounces semisweet chocolate,
   melted

1. In mixer bowl set over hot water, whip eggs with sugar. Heat to 150° (see cake instructions). Remove from heat; beat at high speed until cooled, about 15 minutes.
2. At low speed, add chocolate; beat 5 minutes more.
3. Gradually whip in butter at high speed until frosting stiffens, about 5 minutes. Makes about 3 cups.

MING DYNASTY

Elegant Chinese Dining

Dinner for Six

Fried Oysters

Chicken Corn Soup

Shrimp Stuffed Eggplant

Vegetable Fried Rice

Mandarin Pork Chops

Vegetable Delight

Sesame Glazed Bananas

Jasmine Tea

Beverages:

Chinese Beer or Chardonnay

Timothy Chang, Owner
Fu Shen Chang, Executive Chef

MING DYNASTY

The status of New Chinese (or Nouvelle Chinoise) cuisine in Philadelphia received a boost in 1986 with the opening of Ming Dynasty. Both the food and surroundings here are evocative of fine dining rooms in Hong Kong and Taipei, where the best of traditional Chinese dishes are adapted slightly for European tastes and presentation.

At Ming Dynasty, Timothy Chang and Fu Shen Chang represent the diversity of tastes and viewpoints influencing contemporary Chinese cooking. That this son-father restaurant team has been able to strike a balance between the old and the new, between the cultures of East and West, is in large measure the reason for their restaurant success.

"The colors of a room, the surroundings, affect our appetite. A Chinese restaurant doesn't necessarily have to look like a Chinese temple," says owner Timothy Chang.

Instead, he chose a setting as sophisticated as the dishes selected for the restaurant's elegant script menus. Votive candles are reflected like fireflies off a wall of bevel-edged mirror strips. Soft tones of sand and blue, linen tablecloths, fresh flowers, blue and white patterned china, hot towels and waiters trained in formal French service, all complement the carefully prepared food and set a mood atypical among Chinese restaurants in America.

Unlike most proponents of the New Chinese cooking, Fu Shen Chang approaches the evolving foodstyle from a base of traditional training and Far Eastern experience. He was born and trained in Beijing (Peking), made his way to Taiwan and worked for some years in Taipei before bringing his family to Philadelphia in 1970.

622 South Second Street

FRIED OYSTERS

Oil for deep frying
2½ dozen small shucked
oysters

1 cup CRISPY COATING BATTER
SPECIAL DIPPING SAUCE

1. Heat oil to 325°. Dip oysters in CRISPY COATING BATTER. Oysters should be of uniform size, 2″ to 3″. Drop a few at a time into oil; fry until golden, about 1 minute. Remove with slotted spoon or skimmer; drain.*
2. When ready to serve, heat oil to 350°. Be sure crumbs are skimmed from oil between fryings. Drop prefried oysters in hot oil; fry 1 minute or until crisp and lightly browned. Remove; drain. Serve with SPECIAL DIPPING SAUCE.

Oysters may be prepared 1 hour ahead to this point.

Four deep-fried dishes on a single menu may seem a lot. Each selection here, however, differs in texture and style and shows a side of Chinese cuisine many diners are unaware exists. As with all Chinese cooking, the trick to quick preparation and serving is to have all ingredients chopped and ready to assemble. By using the Chinese chefs' method of double-frying, you can finish all the first fryings, at one temperature, before the meal begins. Serve the rice and vegetable courses with the main dishes and the short cooking breaks between become welcome digestive respites. A temperature-controlled deep fryer simplifies the job; a deep-fry thermometer (to 400°) will do. Or, monitor oil temperature with drops of batter, which take about 2 minutes to turn golden at 325°; about 2 minutes to brown at 350°. When oil is at desired temperature, lower heat slightly to maintain temperature level.

CRISPY COATING BATTER

½ cup flour
½ cup cornstarch

14 tablespoons (⅞ cup) water
¼ teaspoon baking powder

1. Blend all ingredients together in small bowl. Use to coat light foods for deep frying. Makes 1 cup.
2. For BASIC COATING BATTER, add 1 tablespoon each flour and cornstarch to thicken batter.

SPECIAL DIPPING SAUCE

1 cup water	1 tablespoon double black soy
4 tablespoons sugar	sauce
2 tablespoons white vinegar	1 tablespoon dry sherry
	Pinch of salt

Combine all ingredients in bowl or bottle. Use for dipping FRIED OYSTERS, spring rolls, etc. Makes 1¼ cups.

CHICKEN CORN SOUP

4 tablespoons oil	1 teaspoon sugar
3 eggs, beaten	3 tablespoons CORNSTARCH
6 cups CHICKEN BROTH	SLURRY
½ cup cream-style corn	1 boned chicken breast,
	minced

1. In wok or saucepan, heat 3 tablespoons of oil. Scramble fry eggs lightly. Reserve and set aside.
2. In another pan, combine CHICKEN BROTH, corn, and sugar. Bring to a boil. Stir in CORNSTARCH SLURRY. Add chicken and egg. Serve within 30 minutes.

CHICKEN BROTH

2 chicken carcasses	1 gallon water

1. Rinse chicken carcasses (skinless) thoroughly.
2. In stockpot, add carcasses to water; bring to a boil, and simmer for 2 hours. Skim surface residue occasionally. Strain; discard bones. Makes about 3 quarts.

At the restaurant, carcasses are parboiled as a sanitary precaution and the first cooking water discarded along with any residue. The direction above gives home cooks the full flavor of the chicken.

CORNSTARCH SLURRY

To make Cornstarch Slurry: Dissolve cornstarch in an equal measure of water. This liquid blend is more easily incorporated into sauces. Measurements remain the same, as the cornstarch does not measurably increase the volume of the water. Use to tighten or thicken soups or sauces.

SHRIMP STUFFED EGGPPLANT

6 ounces shrimp meat
2 water chestnuts, minced
1 teaspoon minced scallion
2 large (3 small) Chinese
  eggplants

1 cup Basic Coating Batter
Oil for deep frying
SPECIAL BLACK BEAN SAUCE

1. Mince and mash shrimp, or purée. Add water chestnuts and scallion; blend well.
2. Trim ends of long, thin eggplants. Slice a deep cut ¼" in from one end. Do not slice through eggplant. Make second cut ¼" further in and cut through. Repeat. Cut at least 18 pieces, ½" wide, with a "pocket" in the center.
3. Gently spread each "butterflied" piece of eggplant and stuff with shrimp paste.
4. Heat oil to 325°.
5. Coat filled eggplant pieces with Basic Coating Batter. Drop into hot oil, 6 at a time. Fry about 2 minutes or until golden. Remove and drain.*
6. When ready to serve, heat oil to 350°.
7. Drop prefried eggplant into oil in batches. Fry 1 to 2 minutes until crisp and light brown. Remove; drain. Serve Hot.

  * Recipe may be made up to 1 hour ahead to this point.

SPECIAL BLACK BEAN SAUCE

3 tablespoons oil
¾ cup chopped onions
¼ cup chopped mushrooms
¼ cup chopped water chestnuts
½ cup chopped bell peppers,
   mixed red and green

2 teaspoons minced garlic
¼ cup dry sherry
¼ cup salted black beans
¾ cup Chicken Broth
¾ cup CHINESE DARK SAUCE
3 tablespoons Cornstarch
   Slurry

1. In wok or skillet, heat oil. Stir-fry onions, mushrooms, water chestnuts and peppers for 1 minute.
2. Stir in garlic, sherry, black beans, Chicken Broth and CHINESE DARK SAUCE. Bring to a boil.
3. Stir in cornstarch. Serve over Shrimp Stuffed Eggplant or as desired. Makes about 2½ cups.

As with other Chinese dishes, final assembly and cooking of sauce is best done as close to serving time as possible. Store unused salted black beans in oil to keep them soft.

CHINESE DARK SAUCE

1 quart water
¼ cup double black soy sauce
2½ tablespoons sugar

2½ tablespoons sherry
1½ tablespoons salt
1 scallion, chopped fine
½ teaspoon ginger

Combine all ingredients in a container and blend well. Makes 1 quart sauce base.

VEGETABLE FRIED RICE

5 tablespoons oil
3 eggs, beaten
⅓ cup chopped onion
6 ears baby corn, split and cut up
¼ cup chopped mushrooms
¼ cup chopped snowpeas

6 cups cooked rice
1 teaspoon dry sherry
1 teaspoon good sesame oil
1½ teaspoons sugar
¾ teaspoon salt
    Pinch of pepper

1. In large wok or skillet, heat 3 tablespoons of oil. Add eggs, scramble fry; remove and set aside.
2. Heat remaining 2 tablespoons oil. Sauté onion, corn, mushrooms and snowpeas 1 minute. Add rice, sherry, sesame oil, sugar, salt and pepper. Stir-fry to blend and heat through. Stir in reserved egg. Makes about 7 cups.

MANDARIN PORK CHOPS

6 boneless loin pork chops,
  ¾" thick
  MANDARIN MARINADE
2 eggs, beaten

Flour/Cornstarch
Oil for deep frying
MANDARIN SAUCE

1. With a spiked meat mallet, pound chops on both sides to pit surface and reduce to half thickness.
2. Add to *MANDARIN MARINADE*, turning to coat. Let stand 30 minutes, turning occasionally. Drain.
3. Dip pork in beaten egg. Shake or coat with mixture of equal parts flour and cornstarch. Shake off excess.
4. In large skillet, heat oil to 325°. Add chops and remove skillet from heat if chops brown too quickly. Fry about 2 minutes or until chops are almost fully cooked. Remove from heat, drain and set aside.
5. When ready to serve, heat oil to 350°. Refry chops for about 1 minute until hot and crisp. Serve with *MANDARIN SAUCE*.

Those avoiding fried foods may prefer to marinate the pork, skip the coating, and broil the chops. Serve with Mandarin Sauce.

MANDARIN MARINADE

2 tablespoons double black soy
  sauce
2 tablespoons water

2 teaspoons dry sherry
2 teaspoons sugar
Pinch of pepper

Combine all ingredients in shallow bowl and blend well. Makes ⅓ cup marinade for meat or poultry.

MANDARIN SAUCE

6 tablespoons oil
⅓ cup chopped onion
1 tablespoon minced garlic (6
  cloves)
2 tablespoons sugar

⅓ cup Chicken Broth
¾ cup Chinese Dark Sauce
1½ tablespoons Cornstarch
  Slurry

Heat oil in wok or skillet. Sauté onion and garlic. Add sugar, Chicken Broth, Chinese Dark Sauce. Bring to a simmer. Stir in Cornstarch Slurry. Serve with Mandarin Pork Chops or as desired. Makes 1½ cups.

VEGETABLE DELIGHT

3 cups Chicken Broth
2 cups broccoli florets
1 medium carrot, sliced*
1 cup chopped red and green
   bell peppers
1 cup baby corn ears
2 ounces snowpeas
2 ribs bok choy, cut up
1 large rib celery, cut up
½ cup bamboo shoots, cut up
½ cup straw mushrooms

¼ cup sliced white mushrooms
4 water chestnuts, sliced
2 tablespoons oil
1 scallion, chopped
½ teaspoon sugar
½ teaspoon dry sherry
¼ teaspoon sesame oil
  Salt and pepper
1 teaspoon Cornstarch Slurry

1. In wok, bring 2½ cups Chicken Broth to a boil.

2. In bowl, combine broccoli, carrot, peppers, corn, snowpeas, bok choy, celery, bamboo shoots, straw and white mushrooms, water chestnuts. Add to Broth. Cook 1 minute, and stir occasionally. Drain vegetables and set aside. (Broth may be used in soups or for cooking other vegetables.)

3. Heat oil in wok. Sauté scallion.

4. Add remaining ½ cup Chicken Broth, sugar, sherry, sesame oil, salt and pepper. Stir in Cornstarch Slurry. Add reserved vegetables; stir-fry 3 minutes to tender-crisp.

* For visual appeal, use crinkle-cut slicer.

SESAME GLAZED BANANAS

3 or 4 *firm ripe bananas*
　　Basic Coating Batter
　　Oil for deep frying
　1 *cup water*

1½ *cups sugar*
　3 *tablespoons sesame seeds*
　　Ice water

1. Peel and cut chilled bananas in 18 to 24 pieces, 1" wide.
2. Dip bananas in Basic Coating Batter.
3. Heat oil to 325°. Prefry bananas in batches for 2 minutes or until golden. Drain and cool. Reserve.
4. When ready to proceed, heat oil to 340-350°. Refry bananas for 1 to 2 minutes until crisp and lightly browned. Drain; set aside. Have ice water ready.
5. Meanwhile, in wok or skillet on moderate-high heat, combine water and sugar. Boil, stirring continuously, until reduced, thickened and just starting to turn golden, about 4 minutes. Stir in sesame seeds.
6. Add fried bananas, stirring quickly to coat. As sugar begins to brown, move pan off heat. Sugar should be threading by now. Immediately turn coated bananas into ice water to harden glaze. Remove; drain. Serve.

JASMINE TEA

To prepare Jasmine Tea: Place a scant 2 tablespoons of dry Jasmine Tea leaves in the bottom of a 4-cup teapot. Bring a pot of water to a boil and add about 1 cup to the leaves in teapot. Let stand about 5 minutes until leaves open. Fill pot with hot water. Serve hot.

The finest Jasmine Tea, says Chang, comes from the area of Tianjin (Tientsin), Philadelphia's Chinese sister-city.

The Monte Carlo
Living Room

Dinner for Six

Frutti di Mare al Vino Bianco e Zafferano

Ravioloni di Bietole Primavera

Costolette di Vitello all' Aceto Balsamico

Insalata Mista dell' Ortolano al Caprino

Torta di Mascarpone al Limone e Salsa di Fragole Fresche

Espresso

Wines:

With Seafood—Lacryma Cristi Secco, Mastroberardino, 1985
With the Ravioli—Monte Forte Anselmi, 1984
With the Veal—Rubesco Riserva, Lungarotti, 1975
With the Cheese Torte—Moscato d'Asti, Santo Stefan

Umberto degli Esposti, General Manager
Franco Faggi, Manager
Nunzio Patruno, Executive Chef
Giorgio Giuliani, Maitre'd

119

MONTE CARLO LIVING ROOM

Philadelphia's Monte Carlo Living Room, like its jet-set sister club in Monte Carlo, lies between Italy and France in food and mood if not in locale. It's style is Italian with a French accent.

Opened in 1981, the restaurant is operated in partnership by a group of former classmates at Italy's hotel and restaurant management school in Castelfusano. After gaining experience throughout Italy, Monaco and Bermuda, the men decided to pool their talents.

"We wanted to take all the experience we had acquired and put it together in a first-class restaurant that would offer something above everyone else at the same prices," says maitre'd Giorgio Giuliani.

Applying that philosophy to food, chef Nunzio Patruno says everything on the menu must be special. "It has to be, or else it shouldn't be offered," adds Patruno, who was head chef at the Ristorante Polpetta in Monaco.

Why move from Monaco to Philadelphia?

"You have to live in the place where you do business," says Giuliani. "We had been to Philadelphia before and thought we could do well here. It is a calmer atmosphere, more like Europe."

As the hometown of the late Princess Grace, Philadelphia also has close ties to Monaco.

The restaurant is furnished with French velvet and crystal, Milanese lace and Swiss silver and a Leroy Neiman Monte Carlo Casino scene. Upstairs, the lush Living Room lounge, offers one of the city's few dance floors.

In 1985, the group opened the more casual Primavera next door on South Street. Primavera focuses on pastas and earthier dishes.

"We wanted to open a place not too expensive, not too fancy, where the food is genuine," says Giuliani

S.E. Corner of Second and South Streets

FRUTTI DI MARE AL VINO BIANCO E ZAFFERANO

6 small squid, cleaned
 (1 pound)
18 large shrimp
 4 tablespoons butter
18 mussels, scrubbed
18 littleneck clams
 1 shallot, minced

Pinch of saffron threads
¼ cup dry white wine
½ pound sea scallops
 2 cups heavy cream
 Salt and white pepper
 Italian (flatleaf) parsley

1. Slice squid in ¼" rings. Leave tentacles attached to end ring. Shell shrimp, leaving tail attached. Devein. Set aside.
2. Melt butter in skillet, add mussels and clams, cover and cook covered for 8 minutes or until shells open. Add shallot, saffron, wine, shrimp and scallops. Sauté for 2 to 3 minutes.
3. Add cream. Boil to reduce, 2 minutes. Stir in squid; cook 1 to 2 minutes more to thicken sauce.
4. For each serving, arrange 3 shrimp, 3 mussels, 3 clams around a mound of scallops, squid and sauce. Place squid tentacles at center of each. Garnish with parsley.

RAVIOLONI DI BIETOLE PRIMAVERA

½ *recipe PASTA DOUGH*   *PRIMAVERA SAUCE*
  SWISS CHARD FILLING   ¼ *cup grated parmesan cheese*

1. Roll *PASTA DOUGH* in 4 thin sheets, cut 5″ to 6″ wide, 18″ long.
2. Place mounds, 2 to 3 teaspoons, *SWISS CHARD FILLING* in 2 rows, 2″ to 3″ apart, the length of 2 pasta strips.
3. Cover each with a second pasta strip. Press dough together around fillings and cut into 2½″ to 3″ squares.
4. Bring large pot of salted water to a boil. Add ravioli in batches. Cook 1 to 2 minutes after pasta rises to surface. Drain and toss with warm *PRIMAVERA SAUCE*.
5. Serve 4 ravioli with sauce and selected vegetables for each portion. Sprinkle with parmesan cheese.

PASTA DOUGH

1 *pound Semolina flour*   *Pinch of salt*
6 *large eggs*   2 *tablespoons olive oil*

Mix all ingredients together. Knead on floured board. Wrap tightly and refrigerate until ready to use. Makes about 1½ pounds.

SWISS CHARD FILLING

1 *cup blanched Swiss chard,*   2 *tablespoons parmesan cheese*
  chopped (4 ounces raw)   *Pinch of salt and pepper*
½ *cup dry ricotta*   *Freshly grated nutmeg, 2*
2 *eggs, beaten*   *twists of the mill*

Combine all ingredients and mix well. Makes filling for 24 large ravioli. If ricotta is too moist, add 1 to 2 tablespoons of breadcrumbs.

PRIMAVERA SAUCE

24 thin asparagus spears	2 tablespoons butter
1½ pounds mixed seasonal vegetables (baby carrots, broccoli florets, cauliflower florets, trimmed artichokes, fennel, etc)	2 ripe tomatoes, peeled, seeded and chopped
	1 rib celery, chopped or julienned
3 tablespoons chopped onion	1 cup heavy cream
	1 teaspoon chopped basil
	½ teaspoon chopped parsley
	Pinch of salt and pepper

1. Blanch or steam asparagus and chosen vegetables, cut as needed for uniform cooking time to desired crispness. If using artichokes, cut each in half and then in wedges. Keep warm.
2. Sauté onions in butter. Add tomatoes and celery. Cook gently for 5 minutes. Stir in cream, basil, parsley, salt and pepper. Serve with reserved vegetables on pasta.

Fresh ripe tomatoes are preferred for this sauce, but when not available, substitute canned whole tomatoes. If vegetables are cooked and arranged separately, it makes a more attractive plate. Or the vegetables may be sautéed and added to the sauce.

COSTELETTE DI VITELLO ALL' ACETO BALSAMICO

6 veal chops, 1" thick
Flour
Olive oil
Salt and coarse pepper
6 cloves garlic, peeled

1 pint pearl onions, peeled
1½ to 2 cups Balsamic vinegar
6 sprigs rosemary
1 cup VEAL STOCK
4 tablespoons unsalted butter

1. Preheat oven to 375°.
2. Dust veal with flour. Heat an ovenproof pan, add oil and sauté chops, turning once, until just golden. Season with salt and pepper. Add garlic, onions, vinegar and rosemary. Place in 375° oven for 10 minutes.
3. Remove veal and onions from pan. Reserve; keep warm. On stovetop, add VEAL STOCK to sauce and reduce to one third. Whisk in butter to finish.
4. Serve veal topped with sauce, surrounded by onions and accompanied by your choice of garden fresh vegetables.

Veal will be medium-rare if the center feels spongey or springy to the touch. The firmer the feel, the more well done it is.

VEAL STOCK

5 to 6 pounds veal bones
3 carrots, cut up
2 onions, cut up
8 ribs celery, cut up
6 cloves garlic, peeled
3 bay leaves

4 sprigs thyme or 1 teaspoon dried
4 sprigs rosemary or 1 teaspoon dried
2 cups red wine
2 tablespoons tomato paste

1. Brown bones in 400° oven.
2. Have carrots, onions, celery, garlic, bay, thyme, rosemary, red wine and tomato paste ready in stock pot. Add browned bones. Sauté vegetables and bones over medium-high heat for 10 minutes. Add 5 quarts water or more to cover. Bring to a full boil. Reduce to low heat and simmer 5 to 6 hours.
3. Strain. Discard bones and pulp. Return to heat, bring to a boil and reduce to about 2 quarts or desired consistency. Degrease stock.

INSALATA MISTA DELL'ORTOLANO AL CAPRINO

1 small, thin loaf Italian or French bread	3 Belgian endive, leaves separated
½ to ¾ pound goat cheese	2 to 3 tablespoons Balsamic vinegar
6 ounces radicchio	
1 bunch (4 to 6 ounces) arugula	¼ cup extra-virgin olive oil Salt and pepper

1. Slice bread in 12 or 18 slices, about ¼" thick. Top each with a thin slice of cheese. Set aside.
2. Wash greens; pat dry. Toss with vinegar and oil, salt and pepper. Divide dressed greens on plates.
3. Before serving, run bread under a hot broiler for a few minutes to crisp. Serve 2 or 3 slices on each salad.

TORTA DI MASCARPONE AL LIMONE
E SALSA DI FRAGOLE FRESCHE

4 *large eggs, separated*
½ *cup sugar*
2 *cups heavy cream*
    Grated zest of ½ lemon
½ *pound Mascarpone cheese*

1 GÉNOISE, 8″
LEMON SYRUP
CANDIED LEMON PEEL
STRAWBERRY SAUCE

1. Beat egg whites with 2 tablespoons sugar to stiff peaks. Set aside. In another bowl, whip heavy cream. Set aside.

2. Beat egg yolks with remaining 6 tablespoons sugar and lemon zest until light lemon in color. Add cheese and blend well.

3. Fold reserved whites and 3 cups of whipped cream into egg-cheese mixture until smooth and creamy.

4. Slice GÉNOISE horizontally in 3 layers, ½″ each. Place bottom layer on serving plate and moisten with LEMON SYRUP. Spread with one third of Mascarpone cream. Repeat 2 more layers of cake, syrup and cream. Decorate with remaining whipped cream and CANDIED LEMON PEEL.

5. Refrigerate at least 1 hour before slicing. Or freeze, removing 1 hour before serving. Slice carefully and serve on a pool of STRAWBERRY SAUCE.

GÉNOISE

3 *large eggs, at room*
    temperature
⅓ *cup sugar*

1 *teaspoon vanilla extract*
½ *cup sifted flour*
2 *tablespoons melted butter*

1. Heat oven to 350°. Grease and flour an 8″ layer pan.

2. Beat eggs, sugar and vanilla on high for 15 minutes until doubled. If beaten by hand, whisk in bowl set over warm water.

3. Remove from heat, sift flour into egg mixture and fold in gently. Fold in cooled, melted butter.

4. Pour into prepared pan. Bake at 350°, 25 minutes. Cool in pan briefly before turning onto rack to cool.

Génoise batter may be used for madeleines, sponge sheets, petit fours and other cakes.

LEMON SYRUP/CANDIED LEMON PEEL

Julienned peel of 1 lemon   *½ cup sugar*
Water

1. Remove any white pith from peel. Boil peel in 1 cup water about 8 minutes. Strain, reserving water. Rinse peel. Set aside.
2. Add ¼ cup sugar to water and boil until sugar starts to caramelize to a clear golden syrup. Set aside.
3. Heat ½ cup water with remaining ¼ cup sugar. Add reserved peel and boil. Reduce until a thick glaze forms on the peel. Turn peel onto wax paper. Separate and cool.
4. Use peel to decorate, syrup to flavor desserts.

Other types of citrus, such as orange, may be prepared in this way.

STRAWBERRY SAUCE

1 pint strawberries   *2 tablespoons water*
Juice of 1 lemon   *3 tablespoons sugar*
Juice of 1 orange

Purée all ingredients together. Strain. Serve with desserts.

ESPRESSO

Good espresso starts with good coffee beans, roasted dark with a shiny coating of natural oils. A special pot or machine designed to infuse the fine grind with water and steam is essential. Follow directions with the unit. Serve in a demitasse cup. Wipe rim with lemon and dip in raw or brown sugar to garnish. Serve with a twist of lemon peel. Or, spike espresso with your favorite liqueur.

Dinner for Four

Warm Sweetbread Salad Financière

Paella Valenciana

Grand Marnier Ice Cream

Sangria

Wines:

With the Sweetbreads—Corvo Duca Di Salaparuta, 1985
With the Paella—Sangria (see recipe) or the Corvo

Frank and Frances Sanchez, Owners
Frank Sanchez, Executive Chef
Alfredo Staricco, Chef

Pyrenees is one of Philadelphia's many hidden treasures. Since its opening in 1977, there has been almost no publicity or advertising. By word-of-mouth alone, this restaurant has succeeded where so many others fail.

Owner/chef Frank Sanchez is a native "Two Streeter," as lifetime residents of this Second Street South Philadelphia neighborhood are known.

"I worked in this very location as a kid, when it was a grocery store," he recalls of the restaurant's corner site.

In 25 years of hard work, he went from dishwasher at a suburban inn to chef at the old Helen Siegel Wilson's in Center City (where he worked with the late James Beard, Wilson's mentor and menu consultant). Later he opened his own restaurant in Key Largo. But Philadelphia beckoned. And Sanchez came home.

Born of Spanish parents, he was drawn to that ethnic foodstyle. Combining his heritage with his classic kitchen training seemed the natural choice. Thus the Pyrenees menu, like its namesake mountain range, has both French and Spanish influences. The setting is a multi-leveled, stone-walled, Spanish cellar that perfectly complements the food.

Pyrenees two most popular offering—the Paella Valenciana and the Duckling with Chambord Sauce, which Sanchez developed—are representative of the range of Spanish and French dishes among a continental selection which includes cioppina, pork with clams, pasta dishes and occasionally zarzuela. In keeping with trends in the food world, Sanchez expects to put greater emphasis on the Meditteranean styles.

627 South Second Street

WARM SWEETBREAD SALAD FINANCIÈRE

1 pair sweetbread
Flour, optional
Vegetable oil
4 shiitake mushrooms, sliced
½ cup Madeira
½ cup Demi-Glace

4 ounces radicchio
1 Belgian endive
1 small head romaine
LEMON VINAIGRETTE
2 tablespoons minced parsley
QUENELLES

1. Soak sweetbreads (preferably the "gorge" or more rounded half of the pair) in cold water for 3 hours. Poach 10 minutes in water with 1 bay leaf and 4 peppercorns. Drain. Wrap in towel, press with a weight and refrigerate, weighted, overnight.
2. Slice diagonally in ¼" medallions or split into desired portions, depending on the shape and thickness of the sweetbreads. Flour lightly, if desired.
3. Heat oil very hot in skillet. Sear sweetbreads on both sides until lightly crusted. Remove; keep warm.
4. To same pan, add mushrooms, Madeira and Demi-Glace. Bring to a boil. If desired, thin with more Madeira. Add QUENELLES; remove from heat.
5. On each plate, arrange a few leaves of radicchio to the side; 3 leaves of endive with tips dipped in LEMON VINAIGRETTE and chopped parsley; and torn romaine tossed with LEMON VINAIGRETTE. Divide sweetbreads over romaine; top with sauce. Arrange 3 QUENELLES at the side.

LEMON VINAIGRETTE

½ cup vegetable oil
Juice of 1 lemon
1 tablespoon Dijon mustard
1 egg yolk

1 teaspoon minced tarragon or
½ teaspoon dried
Pinch of chopped parsley
Salt and pepper

QUENELLES/FORCEMEAT

1 chicken breast (½ whole)	2 tablespoons heavy cream
1 egg white	Pinch of salt and pepper

1. Skin, bone and remove sinew from chicken.
2. Purée chicken with egg white, cream, salt and pepper in processor. With purée in pastry bag, pipe 1″ florettes into a sauté pan.
3. With care, pour boiling hot water around quenelles to cover. Simmer 2 minutes. Drain. Reserve for garnish.

The same method can be used for quenelles of any size, made with forcemeat of other meats or fish.

PAELLA VALENCIANA

Olive oil, to coat pan	½ pound lean pork, cut up
4 large cloves garlic, minced	4 squid, cleaned, cut in rings
1 cup chopped onion	2 chicken breasts, (1 whole),
1 cup chopped green pepper	boned and cut into chunks
3 or 4 bay leaves	1⅓ cups Chicken Stock or
½ pound (2) Spanish chorizo	bouillon
sausages	12 littleneck clams
1 cup raw rice	12 mussels, scrubbed
2 teaspoons saffron threads	½ cup green peas
12 large shrimp, shelled	12 broccoli florets
and deveined	8 baby carrots
12 sea scallops	¼ cup diced pimiento
4 small lobster tails	
½ pound any firm white fish	
(grouper, monkfish, salmon	
or swordfish), in chunks	

1. Preheat oven to 500°.
2. In large ovenproof skillet, paella pan or cataplana, heat oil. Sauté garlic, onion, green pepper, bay leaves and sausage.
3. Add rice, saffron, shrimp, scallops, lobster tails, fish, pork, squid, chicken and stock. Stir and bring to a boil. Add clams and mussels. Return to a boil. Cover tightly and place in 500° oven for about 15 minutes. You should hear it sizzling. Shells should be opened.
4. Return to stovetop and carefully remove cover.* Add peas, broccoli, carrots and pimiento. Re-cover.
5. Bring back to a boil, remove from heat and set aside 10 minutes (rice will continue to cook). Serve hot.

Don't be intimidated by the long list of ingredients. This is a peasant dish, says Sanchez, thus almost anything might be used or omitted. Also, do not confuse Spanish with Portuguese chorizo, which is spicy.

Paella is often served moist, says Sanchez, but it should not be soupy. If shellfish give off too much liquid, pour a little off into a stock pot. The rice absorbs the rest.

GRAND MARNIER ICE CREAM

4 *egg yolks*
¼ *cup sugar*
1 *ounce Grand Marnier*

¾ *cup heavy cream*
Candied Citrus Peel
(orange)

1. Whip yolks, sugar and liqueur until sugar dissolves and mixture lightens in color.
2. Whip cream to stiff peaks. Fold into yolks. Spoon into chilled, 6 ounce, goblets or freezer container. Freeze.
3. Serve garnished with candied orange peel. Or scoop onto plates painted with puréed, strained, raspberries and garnish with a selection of fresh seasonal fruit pieces.

SANGRIA

2 *ounces Triple Sec*
3 *or more oranges, lemons*
   and/or limes, cut into slices
   or chunks

2 *teaspoons superfine sugar*
1 *ounce brandy*
   Red burgundy
   Club soda or 7-Up

1. Fill a 2-quart pitcher with 5 to 6 cups ice. Add Triple Sec, fruit and sugar. Press fruit with spoon to release flavors.
2. Add brandy. Fill to ¾ with burgundy. Fill with club soda (dry) or 7-Up (sweet), to taste.

"*This is a traditional Spanish sangria, says Sanchez.*

PYRENEES

. . . when you demand the finest!

Raymond Haldeman

Dinner for Six

Escargot with Pasta and Hazelnuts

Spinach and Mushroom Salad with Ginger Coriander Dressing

Grilled Veal Chop with Pistachio Sauce

Baked Mashed Potatoes and Asparagus Bundles

*Bonaparte Pastry Baskets with Raspberries
and Framboise Cream*

Wines:

With the Escargot—Pouilly Fume La Doucette, 1984
With the Veal—Grgich Hills Chardonnay, 1984

Raymond Haldeman, Proprietor and Chef
Triandos Randolph, Chef
Esther Press, Food Consultant

R aymond Haldeman set out to open his namesake restaurant in much the same way he started his own catering business. He just did it. His confidence compensated for the shoestring budget. His knack for pulling in the right people to do any job, not to mention his unlimited powers of persuasion, paid off.

Haldeman started his catering company in 1981 on a $30 bankroll. He chose The Marketplace, Philadelphia's interior design center operations. In a short time, he acquired several trucks, a large staff and one of the busiest schedules in the city. Soon he was called upon to plan menus and prepare dishes for many of the town's top parties, including the annual Beaux Arts ball.

In 1984, Haldeman moved to the Front Street location opposite Penn's Landing and the Delaware River. Working with designer Leslie John Koeser, he turned the space into a setting as stylish as his food. From the chic Tall Ship's Bar to the sunny Fern Room that looks across the courtyard into the glass-walled kitchen, the restaurant is comfortably fashionable.

Haldeman was chef at the popular Garden restaurant in Philadelphia before directing his talents to party planning. From there he travelled up and down the East coast working as catering director aboard the Arara III, a seagoing yacht devoted to corporate entertaining.

When it came time to set up his own restaurant. Haldeman augmented his earlier experience by bringing in an expert, Esther Press. The highly regarded chef and cooking teacher, who helped to open the first DiLullo kitchen, helped to put the new restaurant on track and to instruct new kitchen staffers.

110-112 South Front Street

ESCARGOT WITH PASTA AND HAZELNUTS

½ pound angel hair pasta
(capellini)
1 tablespoon salad oil
6 ounces (1½ sticks) HERB
BUTTER

18 escargot, each cut in half
½ cup skinless hazelnuts,
finely chopped
1½ cups heavy cream
Salt and white pepper

1. In boiling salted water, cook pasta until barely tender, 3 to 4 minutes; strain. Rinse immediately with cold water to stop cooking; drain and toss with oil to avoid sticking. Keep warm in strainer set over hot water.

2. In large sauté pan, over medium heat, melt butter. Sauté escargot and hazelnuts for 5 minutes, until very hot, being careful not to brown butter.

3. Stir in cream. Bring to a boil. Reduce by half, about 5 minutes.

4. Meanwhile, return pasta to hot water for about 1 minute. Drain well. Stir into cream sauce. Adjust seasoning Serve immediately.

Everything can be made in advance, but the final assembly of this dish must be done at the last minute.

HERB BUTTER

1 pound unsalted butter, at
room temperature
2 tablespoons garlic, peeled,
crushed (6 to 8 cloves)

2 tablespoons chopped basil
2 tablespoons chopped parsley
1 tablespoon dill
Salt and white pepper

Combine all ingredients in bowl of processor or blender. Turn onto plastic wrap and, using the wrap, shape into a roll. Or, quarter and shape the butter into 4 small rolls comparable to single sticks of butter. Wrap and freeze.

SPINACH AND MUSHROOM SALAD
WITH GINGER CORIANDER DRESSING

10 ounce bag or ¾ pound fresh
  spinach
½ pound white mushrooms,
  sliced

GINGER CORIANDER
DRESSING
CRACKLINGS or crumbled,
crisped bacon

1. Rinse spinach; drain; pat dry and tear.
2. Toss spinach and mushrooms with GINGER CORIANDER DRESSING. Sprinkle CRACKLINGS over top.

GINGER CORIANDER DRESSING

3 cloves garlic, peeled, crushed
1 tablespoon minced ginger
½ teaspoon sugar
  Salt and pepper
2 tablespoons chopped coriander

Juice of ½ lemon
  (2 tablespoons)
2 tablespoons soy sauce
2 tablespoons red wine
  vinegar
½ cup vegetable or peanut oil

Combine all ingredients in blender or covered container. Blend or shake well. Makes about 1 cup.

CRACKLINGS

To make Cracklings: Preheat oven to 425". Flatten the pieces of poultry skin in a baking sheet with sides to hold rendered fat. Season with salt and pepper. Roast 10 minutes. Drain if needed. Turn skin. Roast 15 minutes more or until well browned, crisp and cooked through. Slice or break into strips or pieces.

GRILLED VEAL CHOPS WITH PISTACHIO SAUCE

6 *loin veal chops, 1" thick*   *VEAL MARINADE PISTACHIO SAUCE*

1. In advance, place veal in pan with *VEAL MARINADE,* turning to coat. Refrigerate at least 2 hours, or overnight, turning occasionally.
2. On high heat, grill veal or sear in very hot ridged skillet, at least 3 minutes on each side for medium-rare.
3. Brush lightly with residual marinade. Serve with PISTACHIO SAUCE in a ramekin on the side.

Press recommends you sear the 1" edges of the meat first, then the bottom and top surfaces to seal in juices. The rarer the meat is to be, the hotter the grill must be. To test for doneness, press gently on meat at center. If meat has a lot of bounce, it is still raw or rare inside. When medium-rare, the meat yields to the touch at the center. As the meat cooks, it gets firmer.

VEAL MARINADE

½ *cup olive oil*   3 *cloves garlic, crushed*
Juice of 1 lemon (¼ cup)   ¼ *teaspoon salt*
4 to 6 *sprigs rosemary, chopped*   ¼ *teaspoon pepper*

Combine all ingredients and use as marinade for veal.

PISTACHIO SAUCE

½ *cup shelled pistachios*   *Pinch of cayenne pepper*
½ *cup heavy cream*   *Salt and white pepper*
½ *teaspoon grated lemon rind*

In blender, grind pistachios fine. Add cream, lemon rind and cayenne. Blend to a thick, mayonnaise-like, consistency. Adjust seasonings. Serve with veal, chicken or white-meat fish. Makes 1 cup.

BAKED MASHED POTATOES

5 medium baking potatoes, peeled	½ to ¾ cup warm milk
2 tablespoons butter	1 clove garlic
½ teaspoon salt	1 tablespoon butter
½ teaspoon white pepper	1 tablespoon grated locatelli cheese
Pinch of grated nutmeg	

1. In water to cover, boil potatoes until soft; drain.
2. In bowl, whip potatoes with butter, salt, pepper, and nutmeg.
3. Gradually whip in as much milk as the potatoes will absorb for desired consistency. These Mashed Potatoes may be served hot as is. Or proceed for Baked Mashed Potatoes.
4. Prepare an 8″ square baking dish by rubbing bottom and sides with cut garlic, then butter.
5. Turn potatoes into dish. Sprinkle cheese over top. Drizzle a spoon or so extra milk over potatoes. Bake at 350° to heat through. Potatoes will form a thin, golden crust.

Mashed Potatoes can be a culinary triumph if done well. Do not prick potatoes during cooking or they will be mealy and wet. Drain potatoes dry before whipping. Do not whip potatoes in a blender. They get gummy.

ASPARAGUS BUNDLES

Trim stems from about 1½ pounds asparagus and steam. Divide and tie in 6 bundles, using long chive leaves as ribbons. At serving time, use tongs to dip bundles briefly in boiling water to reheat. Or, reheat on steamer tray over hot water. Serve drizzled with melted butter and lemon juice. Or, top with buttered breadcrumbs and grated Parmesan cheese and heat on tray in 350° oven for 5 minutes.

BONAPARTE PASTRY BASKETS WITH RASPBERRIES AND FRAMBOISE CREAM

RASPBERRY SYRUP	*FRAMBOISE CREAM*
6 *BONEPARTE PASTRY BASKETS*	1 *pint raspberries*

1. Paint dessert plates with *RASPBERRY SYRUP*. Place 1 *BONEPARTE PASTRY BASKET*, tipped on its side, on each plate.
2. Spoon *FRAMBOISE CREAM* into pastry bag and pipe a continuous swirl or coil of cream into each basket and out onto plate like a spilled cornucopia. Dot raspberries along the cream and around basket. Splash a little *RASPBERRY SYRUP* over cream.

RASPBERRY SYRUP

1 cup sugar	1 pint raspberries, mashed
2 cups water	

Bring sugar and water to a boil. Add raspberries. Simmer 20 minutes; reduce about one-third to syrup. Strain. Makes 2 cups.

BONEPARTE PASTRY BASKETS

3 sheets phylo dough	Confectioners' sugar
Butter, melted	

1. Separate pastry sheets. Brush 1 sheet with butter and sprinkle with confectioners' sugar. Repeat with second and third sheets layering them on top of the first. Do not place sugar on top. Divide dough into 6 squares.
2. Fit phylo into alternating cups of muffin tins. Weight dough with pastry pellets, dry beans, or clean pebbles.
3. Bake at 350°, 5 to 8 minutes until golden. Watch closely. Let cool.

These are best made the same day they will be served.

FRAMBOISE CREAM

1 cup heavy cream	1 tablespoon framboise liqueur
1½ tablespoons confectioners' sugar	½ teaspoon vanilla extract

Combine all ingredients in bowl and beat until cream forms glossy peaks. Makes about 2 cups.

Dinner for Six

Aperitivo Gallo Nero

Ciambella Ai Quattro Formaggi

Risotto Primavera

Sogliola con Ragu D' Astice al Vermouth

Scorzanera e Bietole

Crostata alla Enzo

Wines:

With the Risotto—Grignolino D'Asti
With the Sole—Vernaccia di S. Gimignomo
With the Ricotta Tart —Vin Santo

Enzo and Carla Fusaro, Owners
Carla Fusaro, Executive Chef
Hasan El-Amin, Sous Chef
Enzo Fusaro, Pastry Chef

When Italian-born Enzo and Carla Fusaro opened their Ristorante Il Gallo Nero in 1977, they shared the work and a feeling for good Italian food.

"My husband's philosophy and mine are very similar, that food should be handled as little as possible. I love art, but not on my plate," says Carla Fusaro, who as chef nonetheless turns out some pretty intricate pastas. Half Italian/half French, the redheaded Tuscan admits to being a peasant at heart.

"When it comes to eating, I'm 100 percent Italian. If you have good ingredients, you don't have to smother them with sauces," she adds. "My biggest obsession is fresh ingredients."

Devotion to the purity and integrity of ingredients is part of her Tuscan heritage, she explains. Ingredients need not be expensive, but everything should be fresh and homemade. Fusaro's cooking style is a blend of her grandmother's early teachings and later instruction with noted Italian cooking teacher and cookbook author Giuliano Bugialli. The desserts, however, are left in the expert hands of Enzo Fusaro, a former hotel pastry chef who supplied area restaurants with his "dolce" for 20 years.

The Fusaro's homey blend of the elegant and earthy is reflected in the townhouse dining rooms of the restaurant itself. Italian pottery, an antipasto buffet and piano music wafting from the bar, all are touches that help make Il Gallo Nero a small outpost of Italy in Center City. The restaurant's many expatriot patrons attest to its European style. Together the Fusaros, as hosts, convey to their guests the feeling of being entertained in a private home.

254 South 15th Street

APERTIVO GALLO NERO

Campari   *club soda*
Cointreau   *orange slices for garnish*

In individual cocktail glasses or pitcher, combine equal parts Campari, Cointreau and club soda. Serve over ice. Garnish each drink with an orange slice.

It is unusual for Italians to sip strong cocktails before dinner. This light drink is a specialty of the house.

CIAMBELLA AI QUATTRO FORMAGGI

¼ *pound unsalted butter at room temperature*
¼ *teaspoon salt*
¼ *teaspoon freshly ground pepper*
1 *cup water*
1 *cup all-purpose flour, sifted*
4 *eggs, at room temperature*
¾ *cup freshly grated Gruyere cheese*

¼ *cup freshly grated Parmesan cheese*
¼ *cup freshly grated Pecorino cheese*
¼ *cup freshly grated ricotta Siciliana (a firm ricotta)*
Pinch of freshly grated nutmeg
1 *egg yolk beaten with 1 tablespoon milk*
Slivered almonds or pine nuts

1. Preheat oven to 375°.
2. In heavy saucepan over high heat, combine butter, salt, pepper and water. Bring to a boil. Remove from heat.
3. Add flour all at once. Beat with wooden spoon until mixture is smooth, pulls from pan and forms a ball. Beat over low heat for 1 minute. Let cool 1 minute.
4. Beat in eggs, incorporating each before adding the next. Combine 4 cheeses in bowl. Add 1¼ cups cheese and nutmeg to flour mixture.
5. Mound 12 heaping spoonfuls of pastry in an 8-inch ring on a buttered baking sheet. Glaze with egg/milk mixture. Sprinkle remaining ¼ cup cheese and almonds over top.
6. Bake at 375° for 15 minutes until puffed. Reduce to 350° and bake 45 minutes more until golden brown and firm. Let cool 10 minutes. Serve warm. Makes 12 ciambella.

Chef Fusaro suggests this light hors d'oeuvre be served with the aperitif to "hold" guests while preparing risotto. At Il Gallo Nero, it is a complimentary bar snack.

RISOTTO PRIMAVERA

2 tablespoons oil
¼ pound (1 stick) unsalted butter
¾ pound spinach, stems removed
2 ribs celery, chopped
2 carrots, chopped
1 medium onion, chopped fine
1 bunch parsley, chopped

1 bunch basil, chopped
Salt and pepper to taste
1½ cups arborio rice
Hot Chicken Stock, 2 to 3 cups
¾ cup ITALIAN MEAT SAUCE
Parmesan cheese

1. In saucepan, heat oil and ½ stick butter. Add next 7 ingredients and 3 tablespoons water. Cover and cook gently for 25 minutes.
2. Sauté rice in 2 tablespoons butter for 4 minutes.
3. Purée cooked vegetables and return to saucepan.
4. Add rice to vegetable purée. Add hot stock, ½ cup at a time. Make sure all liquid is absorbed before adding more stock. Do not let it get dry. Cook, stirring often, until rice is barely cooked through and still chewy, about 20 minutes. Risotto should be moist, slightly soupy.
5. Remove from heat. Add ITALIAN MEAT SAUCE. Stir in remaining 2 tablespoons butter. Grate Parmesan cheese into pot, to taste. Stir and turn onto heated platter. Let rest 2 minutes. Serve with additional Parmesan cheese.

Probably the first in Philadelphia to list risotto as a regular menu offering, Carla Fusaro still makes the dish to order for diners patient enough for the 25 minute wait.

ITALIAN MEAT SAUCE

6 tablespoons butter, divided
2 tablespoons olive oil
1 onion, chopped fine
1 carrot, chopped fine
1 rib celery, chopped fine
¼ pound pancetta or Italian
    sweet sausage, chopped fine

6 ounces lean ground pork
6 ounces lean ground beef
½ cup dry red wine
1 tablespoon tomato paste
½ cup Brown Stock or beef
    bouillon
Salt and pepper

1. In skillet, heat 3 tablespoons butter with oil. Add onion, carrot, celery and pancetta (salted, unsmoked, bacon); cook on low heat until vegetables soften.
2. Add pork and beef. Crumble and fry gently until meat starts to brown. Add wine; cook off liquid.
3. Dilute tomato paste with 2 tablespoons Brown Stock; stir into sauce. Cover; reduce heat to low and stir often. Gradually add remaining 6 tablespoons stock. Total cooking time is 1½ hours.
4. Stir in remaining 3 tablespoons butter to finish the dish. Serve with risotto or pasta. Makes about 1 quart.

SOGLIOLA CON RAGU D'ASTICE AL VERMOUTH

6 Dover sole, pan dressed,
    skinned, 8 ounces each
3 chicken lobsters, 1 to 1¼
    pounds each
¼ cup olive oil
¼ pound (1 stick) butter
3 cloves garlic
1 medium carrot, cut in rounds
½ pound celeriac, sliced thin
2 leeks, chopped fine

¼ cup Cognac
¼ cup dry Vermouth
1 cup white wine
3 ripe tomatoes, skinned,
    seeded and cubed
6 tablespoons chilled butter,
    in cubes
1 pint heavy cream
30 fresh tarragon leaves
    Salt and white pepper

1. Dress and skin sole if fishmonger has not done so. Set aside.
2. Put lobsters in boiling water. Return to a boil; cook 5 minutes. Drain. Split; remove tail and claw meat. Cut into medallions. Set aside. (Save the green tomally to use as a spread and the shell for stock).
3. Break up carcasses and sauté in oil 15 minutes on high flame. Add ½ stick butter, garlic, carrots, celeriac and leeks; sauté 15 minutes more.
4. Add Cognac; flame. Add vermouth and white wine. Cook gently 20 minutes to reduce by one-third. Strain in fine sieve and remove the shell. Add tomatoes and cook 10 minutes more.
5. Slice and add reserved lobster; heat 3 minutes.
6. Remove from heat; remove meat and keep warm.
7. Whisk butter cubes into sauce, one at a time. Add cream and reduce by one-third. Add tarragon, salt, and pepper.
8. Sauté sole in remaining ½ stick butter. Carefully remove center bones. Stuff with reserved lobster meat. Spoon sauce on hot platter. Serve stuffed sole on sauce.

Italians prepare and serve fish with the head intact to assure freshness. But you can present the dish with the head removed.

SCORZANERA E BIETOLE

To prepare Salsify: Peel 1 pound salsify root; cut in julienne sticks. (Save stems for other use.) Boil in water with 1 tablespoon lemon juice, 5 minutes. Drain. Toss with Balsamic vinegar and olive oil. Serve at room temperature.

To prepare Swiss Chard: Wash 2 pounds chard; trim stems (save for other use). Blanch; drain; chop. Sauté in olive oil with 1 teaspoon minced garlic. Serve warm.

Vegetables served at room temperature are an Italian tradition.

CROSTATA ALLA ENZO

PASTA FROLLA (Short Pastry)
¾ *pound ricotta, well drained*
1 *cup PASTRY CREAM*
6 *tablespoons sugar*
1 *egg yolk*

¼ *teaspoon vanilla extract*
Grated rind of 1 lemon
VANILLA SUGAR
White grapes for garnish

1. Roll *PASTA FROLLA* and line a tart pan, 10"x 1" deep. Prick bottom with fork. Bake 10 minutes at 300°.

2. In mixing bowl, whip ricotta and *PASTRY CREAM* for 2 minutes. Add sugar, egg yolk, vanilla and lemon rind; mix 1 minute more. Turn into partially baked pastry shell.

3. Bake at 400° for 25 minutes. Let cool. Serve with a sprinkling of *VANILLA SUGAR* and garnish of white grapes.

Enzo created this recipe for a ricotta tart made in the Florentine style. It can be made ahead, but dries quickly once cut. Use within two days. Serve at room temperature.

PASTA FROLLA (SHORT PASTRY)

¾ *pound (3 sticks) unsalted*
   butter, at room temperature
1¼ *cups confectioners'*
   sugar
   Pinch of salt

2 *eggs at room temperature*
5 *cups cake flour*
5 *ounces almonds, toasted and*
   chopped very fine

1. In bowl, blend butter, sugar and salt for 4 minutes at medium speed. Add eggs, one at a time. Beat 3 minutes.

2. Combine cake flour and almonds. Beat flour/nut mix into butter gradually at low speed. Chill 2 hours. Divide to use or freeze. Makes pastry for 2 large tarts.

Almonds should be ground almost to a flour consistency but not to a paste. Roll trimmings in thin strips, arrange lattice pattern over tart.

PASTRY CREAM

1¼ cups sugar
¾ cup cake flour
¼ teaspoon vanilla extract

Pinch of salt
1 quart warm milk
6 large egg yolks

1. In mixing bowl, combine sugar, flour, vanilla and salt. Stir in 1 cup milk and egg yolks. Whisk briskly for 1 minute. Gradually whip in remaining 3 cups milk.
2. Transfer to heavy enamel or stainless steel saucepan, and bring milk slowly to a simmer, stirring steadily. Reduce heat very low and cook, stirring, for 2 minutes. (Or move pan over hot water to finish cooking.) Store covered closely to prevent surface skin from forming. Makes 5 cups.

VANILLA SUGAR

To make Vanilla Sugar: Bury 1 vanilla bean in jar with 1 pound granulated sugar for a week or more.

SANSOM STREET OYSTER HOUSE

SEAFOOD SINCE 1947

Dinner for Four

Marinated Mussel Salad

Shrimp Bisque

Rainbow Trout with Oyster Stuffing

Deep Dish Apple Pie with Vanilla Sauce

Wines:

With the Mussels and Bisque—Domaine Chandon Brut
With the Trout—Chardonnay "Laforet", Joseph Drouhin, 1984
With the Apple Pie—Gewurtztraminer Late Harvest

David Mink, Owner
Cleveland General, Chef

155

F ish and seafood are as much a part of the Philadelphia foodstyle as they are in towns like Boston and San Francisco, towns better known for their ports and proximity to fishing areas. And nowhere is that seafood fresher, the oysters plumper or presentation simpler than at the Sansom Street Oyster House.

With the Oyster House, owner David Mink is continuing a family seafood house tradition begun by his father in 1947.

"Some people are born with a silver spoon in their mouths; I had an oyster fork," quips Mink, who opened on Sansom Street in 1976.

The restaurant's policy is as straightforward and simple at that of the early Philadelphia oyster houses: Offer good, fresh food inexpensively.

"We've always served the freshest seafood at reasonable prices," says Mink.

Recent renovations added a second dining room, a cocktail bar and an oyster bar. "We tried to recreate the atmosphere of our old oyster house," he says of the newly traditional decor.

The "raw bar" features the popular Belon oysters, an imported delicacy the Mink family is believed to have introduced to Philadelphia, and Chincoteagues from nearby waters.

The warmth of the brass-railed oak bars, the oak furnishings and panelling, and other turn-of-the-century detailing softens the stark simplicity of traditional tile flooring and reminds long-time patrons of Sansom Street's predecessor and the family's original seafood house Kelly's on Mole Street. The family's extensive collection of antique and unusual oyster plates is represented, in part, by the roughly 250 pieces on display throughout the restaurant.

1516 Sansom Street

MARINATED MUSSEL SALAD

4 pounds mussels,
   4 to 5 dozen
6 cloves garlic, minced
½ cup extra-virgin olive oil
½ cup dry white wine

¼ cup chopped pimiento
2 tablespoons minced parsley
   Dash of white pepper
½ pound lettuce or other
   seasonal salad greens

1. From 2 to 24 hours in advance, scrub mussels, removing beards. In pot with 1″ boiling water, poach mussels until shells open, 5 to 10 minutes. Let cool. Remove mussel meat from shells; reserve.
2. Sauté garlic in 4 tablespoons of oil.
3. In mixing bowl, combine garlic oil, remaining oil, wine, pimiento, parsley and pepper. Add mussels; toss to coat. Marinate, refrigerated, for 2 hours. Serve on shredded or leaf lettuce.

SHRIMP BISQUE

1 pound medium shrimp	Pinch of thyme
1 quart water	Pinch of cayenne pepper
2 ribs celery, cut up	Salt and white pepper
½ Spanish onion, cut up	1 cup light cream
1 medium carrot, cut up	1 tablespoon flour blended
4 tablespoons (½ stick) butter	with ½ cup water
1 bay leaf	Medium-bodied sherry

1. Shell shrimp; rinse, de-vein and reserve. Boil shells in water for 15 minutes. Strain; discard shells.

2. To broth, add celery, onion, carrot, butter, bay leaf, thyme, and cayenne. Simmer for 1 hour; strain. Remove bay leaf. Purée vegetables and return to stock.

3. Stir in cream; cook 10 minutes. Add salt and pepper to taste. Add the "white wash" of flour and water to "tighten" liquid; simmer 5 minutes. Or, reduce on low heat.

4. Shortly before serving, add reserved raw shrimp cut in 1" pieces. Cook 3 minutes. Let guests add their own sherry, about 1 teaspoon per serving. Makes about 1 quart.

RAINBOW TROUT WITH OYSTER STUFFING

4 *dressed Rainbow trout*
(brook trout), about 12
ounces each

OYSTER STUFFING
Oil
Paprika

1. Rinse fish; pat dry. Preheat broiler, about 500°.
2. Spoon about ¾ cup OYSTER STUFFING into each fish. Close.
3. With sharp knife, make a 3″ slit, lengthwise, through upper fillet to vent steam and allow stuffing to expand.
4. Brush broiler pan with oil. Sprinkle paprika over fish and broil for 3 minutes, until browned. Transfer pan to oven for 4 to 6 minutes more, at 500°, to finish cooking.

OYSTER STUFFING

1 *pint select oysters*
2 *tablespoons butter*
½ *small green bell pepper,*
   seeded and chopped
2 *tablespoons chopped onion*
2 *tablespoons chopped celery*
1 *scallion, chopped*
1 *chicken liver and 1 gizzard*
   (or 2 livers), chopped

1 *tablespoon minced parsley*
⅛ *teaspoon ground bay leaves*
   Pinch of thyme
   Pinch of mace
   Pinch of cayenne pepper
2 or 3 *slices day-old French bread,*
   cubed

1. Drain oysters; cut in 1″ pieces and set aside; Reserve liquor.
2. In small skillet, heat butter and sauté green pepper, onion, celery and scallion for 1 minute. Add chicken liver, gizzard, parsley, bay, thyme, mace and cayenne. Sauté for 2 minutes.
3. In mixing bowl, stir together vegetables, oysters, bread and a little oyster liquor, if desired, to moisten. Makes about 3 cups stuffing.

Mink adapted this stuffing from a recipe in his well-worn copy of friend Howard Mitchum's cookbook, Creole Gumbo and All That Jazz (Addison Wesley Publishing; 1980).

DEEP DISH APPLE PIE WITH VANILLA SAUCE

4 McIntosh apples
2 teaspoons lemon juice
4 teaspoons sugar
4 teaspoons instant dissolving
½ flour
¼ teaspoon cinnamon
   teaspoon nutmeg

½ cup apple cider
4 teaspoons orange juice
4 teaspoons Apple Jack brandy
1 tablespoon butter
PIE CRUST PASTRY
VANILLA SAUCE

1. Peel, core and slice apples; toss with lemon juice.
2. Combine sugar, flour, cinnamon and nutmeg.
3. Combine cider, orange juice and Apple Jack. Add sugar mixture; stir to dissolve. Add apples; mix well.
4. Divide filling between 4 oven-proof dishes, 1 cup each, or place in 1½-quart baking dish. Dot with butter.
5. On floured surface, roll PIE CRUST PASTRY thin and bit over filling in baking dishes. With sharp knife, make a few slits in pastry to vent steam.
6. Bake at 350° for 20 minutes, until bubbly and brown. Serve hot with warm VANILLA SAUCE.

PIE CRUST PASTRY

1 cup all-purpose flour
½ teaspoon salt

⅓ cup solid vegetable
   shortening, chilled
2 to 3 tablespoons cold water

1. In mixing bowl, stir together flour and salt.
2. Cut in shortening. Add water gradually while mixing with fork, using just enough to form dough.
3. Pat dough into a ball; flatten and roll between sheets of waxed paper or on floured surface to desired size. Makes pastry for a single crust 9" pie or for 4 individual (5") pies.

VANILLA SAUCE

1 cup milk
1 tablespoon sugar
½ teaspoon vanilla extract

¼ teaspoon butter
1 teaspoon cornstarch
   dissolved in 1 teaspoon
   water

Bring milk to a boil; add sugar, vanilla, butter and cornstarch slurry. Whisk over low heat until thickened. Makes about 1 cup.

Dinner for Four

*Grilled Peppers and Zucchini with Goat Cheese
and Caper Vinaigrette*

*Tomato-Basil Pasta
with Petite Snails and Zinfandel Sauce*

*Lobster with Thai-Coriander Cream Sauce
and Cellophane Noodles*

Terrine of Three Chocolates

Wines:

*Chateau Montelena, 1982, Napa Valley Zinfandel
Jordan, 1982, Alexander Valley Chardonnay*

*Steven Poses, Owner
Carol DeLancey, Restaurant Manager
Herb Gunther, Executive Chef*

163

T he 16th Street Bar & Grill occupies the same storefront location that had been the home to its sister restaurant Frög since 1973. It took a while, however, for the simple, neighborhood grill, opened in 1981, to shift its menu more towards the innovative dishes that made Frög famous.

It was in the early, funky days of Frög that the blend of French, Thai and American ingredients and techniques now known as Philadelphia Cuisine evolved. Owner/Chef Steve Poses was introduced to the French/Far Eastern style behind the scenes at the late Le Panetière. His co-worker there, Kamol Phutlek, later became chef at Frög.

Frög moved to a larger, more elegant location in 1980, having inspired a new era of dining in Philadelphia. it became the cornerstone of Poses' fast-growing food service empire—Shooting Stars, Inc.—which now includes Frög/Commissary Catering, the Commissary (a gourmet cafeteria), The Market at the Commissary (for gourmet provisions and takeout) and the USA Cafe (with American regional fare).

The mature Frög "retired" in 1987, but the creativity of its chefs is captured in The Frög/Commissary Cookbook (Doubleday & Co.; 1985), and co- authored by Poses, Ann clark and Becky Roller.

And at 16th Street, in the same kitchen where it all began 14 years ago, the early Frög spirit is being recaptured with food, great desserts, an exciting wine list and moderate prices. Frög, with its umlaut "eyes," took a light- hearted, light-handed tack with French food. At 16th Street, Mediterranean influences now prevail. And the option of smaller portions lets you sample a wide range of dishes.

"Our approach has always been that borders and traditions count less than flavors," said Poses. "In the past, France provided much of the inspiration along with Far Eastern cuisines, particularly Thai. At 16th Street, the palette of Southern Italian and Mediterranean cuisines now plays a larger part."

264 South 16th Street

GRILLED PEPPERS AND ZUCCHINI WITH GOAT CHEESE AND CAPER VINAIGRETTE

3 *Red bell peppers*	1 *cup cooked white beans*
Olive oil	1 *cup* CAPER VINAIGRETTE
4 *small zucchini, trimmed, cut*	4 *slices goat cheese, about 3*
lengthwise in 4 slices	*ounces each*
	chopped parsley for garnish

1. Brush peppers with oil. Roast over flame or at 475° until skin is charred. Cool. Peel and seed peppers. Cut in ½-inch strips and dice. Mix peppers and beans. Refrigerate.
2. Brush zucchini slices with oil. Grill or saute until crisp- tender.
3. Combine pepper/bean mixture with ¾ cup of CAPER VINAIGRETTE. Mound, divided evenly, on 4 salad plates.
4. Toss zucchini slices lightly in 2 tablespoons CAPER VINAIGRETTE. Arrange 4 slices on each plate by beans.
5. Add a slice of goat cheese to each plate. Spoon about ½ tablespoon CAPER VINAIGRETTE on each cheese slice. Garnish with chopped parsley.

CAPER VINAIGRETTE

1½ *cups extra virgin olive oil*	4 *anchovy fillets*
½ *cup red wine vinegar*	2 *cloves garlic*
4 *tablespoons capers, drained*	2 *eggs*
2 *tablespoons Dijon mustard*	*Salt and pepper*

1. In processor or blender, combine oil, vinegar, capers, mustard, anchovies and garlic. Blend until smooth.
2. Add eggs. Blend until thickened. Season with salt and pepper to taste. Refrigerate. Makes about 2 cups.

TOMATO **PASTA WITH PETITE SNAILS AND ZINFANDEL SAUCE**

5 ounces smoked bacon or salt
   pork, cut in ½-inch dice
12 shallots, peeled
¼ pound (1 stick) unsalted
   butter
2 cups Zinfandel wine

½ pound TOMATO BASIL PASTA
8 shiitake or other wild
   mushrooms, cut in half
4 tablespoons butter
24 petite snails
1 cup ZINFANDEL SAUCE
   Salt and pepper

1. In oven or broiler, roast bacon pieces at 400°-500° until brown and crisp and drained of fat. Reserve.
2. In saucepan, brown shallots in ½ stick butter. Add 1 cup wine; cook until tender, about 10 minutes. Set aside.
3. In strainer set in boiling water, cook TOMATO BASIL PASTA until just cooked through. Keep warm over hot water.
4. In skillet, saute mushrooms briefly in remaining ½ stick butter. Add snails; cook for 1 minute. Add remaining 1 cup wine, ZINFANDEL SAUCE, reserved shallots in wine and reserved bacon lardoons or cracklings. Bring to a simmer. Season with salt and pepper, to taste.
5. Mound cooked pasta on warmed plates. Arrange 6 snails around each mound. Ladle Zinfandel Sauce over pasta.

TOMATO BASIL PASTA

1 cup flour
1 large egg

1½ teaspoons minced basil
1 tablespoon tomato puree

1. In processor bowl, combine flour, egg, basil and tomato puree. Process 10 seconds, until crumbly. Dough should form a ball when squeezed together. If too dry add more puree or water, 1 teaspoon at a time.

2. Turn onto lightly floured surface. Form ball and knead briefly until smooth.

3. Using pasta machine or by hand, roll and cut dough to desired widths. Start at widest setting and gradually roll dough thinner. Spread pasta on lightly floured surface and dust with flour, semolina or cornmeal. Makes ½ pound.

ZINFANDEL SAUCE

4 cups Brown Sauce	1 sprig fresh thyme or 2
2 small shallots, minced	tablespoons dried
3 cups Zinfandel wine	2 bay leaves

In saucepan, combine Brown Sauce, shallots, wine, thyme and bay leaves. Cook over high heat until reduced by half, about 30 minutes. Strain. Makes about 3½ cups.

LOBSTER WITH THAI-CORIANDER CREAM SAUCE AND CELLOPHANE NOODLES

4 lobsters (1½ pounds each) or 4 lobster tails
2 tablespoons butter
2 teaspoons Thai green curry paste
4 slices fresh ginger
4 loves garlic, peeled and lightly crushed
4 ounces chanterelles or other exotic mushrooms, sliced
2 cups heavy cream infused with a pinch of saffron

Juice of ½ lime, about 1 tablespoon
1 cucumber, halved and seeded
10 snowpeas, cut diagonally in triangles
Salt and white pepper
2 cups cellophane noodles (4 ounces dry), softened in warm water
2 tablespoons minced chives
4 tablespoons coriander leaves

1. In advance, shell lobsters. Cut tails in half lengthwise. Pick out claw and arm meat. Reserve, refrigerated. (Use shells for seafood stock, if desired.)

2. In sauté pan, heat butter, curry paste, ginger, garlic and mushrooms. Add cream; simmer until reduced by a third, about 30 minutes. Remove ginger, garlic; discard.*

3. When ready to serve, reheat sauce and add reserved lobster meat. Add lime juice, cucumber balls and snowpea triangles. Heat through. Season with salt and pepper.

4. Reheat noodles in hot water. Drain. Serve to the side on warmed plates. Arrange lobster pieces, with sauce, next to noodles. Garnish with chives and coriander leaves. Serve accompanied by steamed broccoli florettes, if desired.

Recipe may be prepared in the morning to this point.

TERRINE OF THREE CHOCOLATES

3¾ cups heavy cream
½ cup CRÈME FRÂICHE or
    sour cream
12 egg yolks
¾ cup sugar
1½ cups Half & Half
3 vanilla beans, scraped
1 tablespoon prepared espresso
    coffee

2 ounces white chocolate,
    chopped
1 tablespoon malt powder
2 ounces milk chocolate,
    chopped
2 ounces bittersweet chocolate,
    chopped

1. Whip 2¼ cups heavy cream until thickened. Add CRÈME FRAÎCHE. Whip until soft peaks form. Set aside.

2. Butter a 6-cup loaf pan. Line with waxed paper.

3. Whip 4 yolks with ¼ cup sugar until it forms a ribbon.

4. In heavy saucepan, combine ½ cup heavy cream, ½ cup Half & Half and vanilla bean. Bring to boiling.

5. Remove from heat. Add coffee and white chocolate. Stir to melt chocolate. Turn into mixer bowl. Whip at medium speed until cool and mousse- like, about 10 minutes.

6. Refrigerate until cold. Fold in 1½ cups reserved whipped cream. Turn into prepared loaf pan; freeze.

7. For second layer, repeat steps Nos. 3 to 6, except that additions in step No. 5 are malt and milk chocolate.

8. For third layer, repeat steps Nos. 3 to 6, except that addition in step No. 5 is bittersweet chocolate only.

9. Place assembled terrine in the freezer for at least 6 hours or overnight. Before serving, unmold and remove waxed paper. To serve, slice with a hot knife. Serve, if desired, with Creme Anglaise, Chocolate Citrus Sauce or a fruit sauce.

CRÈME FRAÎCHE

1 *cup heavy cream*   2 *tablespoons lemon juice (lemon)*
1 *tablespoon buttermilk*

1. In stainless steel bowl, mix cream and buttermilk. Heat slightly (85). Cover; let stand in warm (75) place 12 hours or until thickened. Drain. Chill for 24 hours before using. Keeps up to 2 weeks, refrigerated. Makes 1 cup.

2. For next batch, use Crème Fraîche for buttermilk.

Dinner for Four

Fresh Lotus Salad with Go Chi and Scallop Dressing

Lobster Pear

Salmon with Black Bean Sauce

Duck with Shiitake Mushrooms and Young Ginger

Fresh Fruit

Wines:

With the Lobster—Robert Mondavi Johannisberg Riesling, 1984
With the Salmon—Kenwood Chardonnay, 1983
With the Duck—Sutter Home Zinfandel, 1984

E-Hsin and Susanna Foo, Proprietors
Susanna Foo, Executive Chef

I t's not just the tablecloths, fresh flowers, and tuxedo-clad waiters that make Susanna Foo Chinese Cuisine different from other Chinese eateries. This is an uptown restaurant where East meets West head-on in the kitchen.

Owner/chef Susanna Foo, in developing her own innovative style of New Chinese cooking, has become a leading proponent of this fast-rising foodstyle. The ingredients, the tastes and textures, are Chinese, but the methods of preparation are often French. Menu selections range from the traditional Kung Pao Chicken to a more contemporary roasted duck with Belgian endive and spicy mustard dressing. The menu mingles the familiar with the unexpected, including salads like the fresh lotus, go chi and scallop combination presented here. Diners also may request dishes prepared along Pritikin guidelines.

"In French restaurants they always use onion, celery and carrots, while the Chinese use just a little ginger and scallion," says Foo, who has created several flavorful stock bases using Chinese seasonings in French-style reductions. "All our spices are Chinese and we use a lot of Chinese ingredients, but with the French technique."

The restaurant opened in 1979, under the hame Hu-Nan, in an impressively appointed building that had been a private club. It moved to its current, more central, location in the fall of 1987.

With the move, the Foos decided the timing was right for switching to a name that better reflects the contemporary style of the restaurant.

"There are so many Hunan restaurants," says Foo. "It was confusing. We even got calls for take-out."

1512 Walnut Street

FRESH LOTUS SALAD WITH GO CHI
AND SCALLOP DRESSING

This salad is pleasing to both the eye and the palate. Its brilliant scarlet berries contrast with the creamy white lotus root. The combination is sweet, spicy and crunchy.

1 pound fresh lotus root	SCALLOP DRESSING
1 tablespoon lemon juice	1 Belgian endive (24 leaves)
1 tablespoon go chi, plumped in water	1 tablespoon minced coriander or mint
4 ounces mâche (lamb's lettuce) or watercress	

1. Peel and slice lotus root very thin. Place slices in bowl with lemon juice. Stir to coat. Add drained go chi and mâche. Refrigerate, covered, until serving time.

2. At serving time, toss reserved lotus salad in bowl with SCALLOP DRESSING. Arrange lotus and lettuce on plates with 6 spokes of endive. Garnish with go chi and coriander.

Fresh lotus root, available from September through January, is carried by some Asian groceries here. The root looks rather like a long radish and should be peeled. Like a potato, the flesh turns brown when exposed to the air. Always coat lotus root with lemon juice or citric acid. If fresh root is not available, fresh water chestnuts (available year round) are the preferred substitute.

Go chi are bright red berries, similar to currants. They are cultivated in China and sold, dried, in Asian groceries. They are often used to enrich the nutritional value of broths. Substituting currants for go chi lacks the color but is close for taste. Or, use diced red pepper or pimiento.

SCALLOP DRESSING

2 large Chinese dried scallops (or 4 medium)
3 tablespoons olive oil
1 tablespoon white wine vinegar

1 teaspoon minced ginger
¼ teaspoon salt
Pinch of pepper

1. Soak dried scallops in water overnight to soften. Shred and drain. (Add liquid to a seafood stock).
2. Combine remaining ingredients in bowl or covered container. Add scallops. Blend well. Chill for several hours to meld flavors.

Dried scallops, available in Asian groceries in 4 and 8 ounce packages, are rather expensive. Dried shrimp, if on hand, may be substituted, says Foo. For a lighter, milder dressing, use cooked fresh scallops.

LOBSTER PEAR

6 large fresh sea scallops
1 tablespoon oil
1 tablespoon gin
   Pinch of salt
3 ripe pears, peeled
   LOBSTER STUFFING

12 sticks, ¼" x ¼" x 1", smoked Virginia ham (2 ounces)
1 tablespoon go chi or ¼" diced red pepper
12 leaves fresh coriander
   SHRIMP SAUCE, heated

1. In advance, rinse scallops; pat dry. Slice each horizontally in rounds, ¼" thick. Combine with oil, gin and salt. Set aside to marinate at least 15 minutes.
2. Core pears; cut in half from stem. With cut sides down, stamp out a 1¼" circle from each half with cookie cutter (preferably scalloped). Slice 2 rounds from the circle, ¼" to ⅓" thick from each circle to make 12 rounds. (Trimmings may be used in fruit dessert).

3. Assemble by topping each pear round with *LOBSTER STUFFING*. Cover each with a round of raw scallop. Secure by poking a ham stick down into center of each piece. On each, place garnish of 2 or 3 go chi berries.

4. In steamer over hot water, steam 12 Lobster Pear pieces over high heat for about 5 minutes, until lobster filling and scallop become firm and opaque. Do not overcook.

5. For each serving, arrange 3 Lobster Pears on warm plate. Top with coriander. Spoon a little *SHRIMP SAUCE* over each.

LOBSTER STUFFING

1 *medium egg white*	1 *teaspoon minced fresh*
2 *tablespoons ground loin*	*ginger or ¼ teaspoon*
pork fat	*ground*
1 *tablespoon minced coriander*	¼ *teaspoon salt*
stems	¼ *teaspoon white pepper*
1 *tablespoon gin or vodka*	2 *South African lobster tails,*
1 *teaspoon good sesame oil*	*about 7 ounces each*

1. Combine all ingredients except lobster in bowl and set aside.

2. Up to 2 hours before assembling dish, remove meat from lobster tails; cut lobster in small pieces. Combine meat and reserved binder; mix well. Use immediately or refrigerate for up to 2 hours.

Use sesame oil that is neither too light ("no taste") nor too dark ("too strong"). It should be brownish in color. The best, says the chef, comes from Japan.

SHRIMP SAUCE

¼ cup soybean oil
½ cup diced onion
½ cup dry white wine or sake
2 cup chopped fresh tomato
2 tablespoons Chinese dried
   shrimp, ground

1 teaspoon freshly ground
   pepper
2 cups CHINESE SHRIMP
   STOCK or Chicken Stock
1 tablespoon Cornstarch
   Slurry
   Salt to taste

1. Heat oil in saucepan; sauté onion to light brown.
2. Add wine, tomato, dried shrimp, pepper and SHRIMP STOCK; bring to a boil. Simmer 20 minutes or until mixture reduces by one third. Strain, discard pulp, and adjust seasoning.

This sauce is salty and gets stronger as it is reduced. The stronger the flavor, the less sauce is needed to accent the mild Lobster Pear medallions.

CHINESE SHRIMP STOCK

5 cups Chicken Broth or Stock
2 tablespoons dried shrimp or
   1 cup shrimp shells

1 star anise
1 teaspoon ginger peelings
½ teaspoon green peppercorns

Combine all ingredients in saucepan. Bring to a boil, simmer one half hour or until stock is reduced by 1 cup. Strain. Makes 1 quart.

SALMON WITH BLACK BEAN SAUCE

1 *fillet of salmon, 10 ounces*
6 *ounces spinach leaves*

½ *red bell pepper, cored,*
  seeded and julienned
  BLACK BEAN SAUCE

1. Cut salmon into 12 strips, about 1" wide, and place on a lightly oiled dinner plate. Place into covered steamer and cook over simmering water, about 5 minutes. Divide spinach on serving plates.
2. Arrange salmon on spinach beds. Top each strip with red pepper. Spoon BLACK BEAN SAUCE over fish.

BLACK BEAN SAUCE

3 *tablespoons soybean oil*
2 *cloves garlic, crushed*
1 *piece ginger, 2" by ½", mashed*
2 *tablespoons fermented black beans*
½ *cup dry white wine*

1 *cup Fish Stock or Chicken Stock*
1 *teaspoon Szechuan peppercorns*
½ *teaspoon white pepper*
½ *teaspoon sugar*
1 *teaspoon Cornstarch Slurry Salt*

1. Heat oil in saucepan. Add garlic, ginger and black beans; cook until lightly browned. Add wine; cook for 5 minutes. Add Fish Stock, peppercorns, pepper, sugar and Cornstarch Slurry; bring to a boil. Reduce sauce by one half.
2. Strain sauce, reserving whole black beans. Return beans to strained sauce or keep separate as garnish. Salt to taste. Keep warm for serving. Makes ½ to ¾ cup.

DUCK WITH SHIITAKE MUSHROOMS AND YOUNG GINGER

*Boned breast meat of 2
ducks, about 1½ pounds*
DUCK MARINADE
½ *cup soybean oil*
1 *ounce fresh young ginger,
peeled and sliced thin*

3 *ounces Shiitake mushrooms*
1 *hot red pepper, sliced thin*
¼ *red bell pepper, seeded and
julienned*
HU-NAN DUCK SAUCE
Cooked white rice

1. Cut duck meat, diagonally across grain, in slices ¼" thick. Stir in DUCK MARINADE; let stand 10 minutes.
2. Drain marinade from duck. In wok, heat 6 tablespoons oil. Add duck slices and stirfry just until barely cooked, 2 to 3 minutes. Remove and set aside.
3. Add remaining 2 tablespoons oil to wok. Sauté ginger, mushrooms and hot red pepper until mushrooms soften.
4. Return duck to wok. Add HU-NAN DUCK SAUCE. On high heat, cook 1 to 2 minutes more. Serve on warm plates, accompanied by cooked white rice.

This dish is based on Cantonese duck with young ginger. Chef Foo adapted it, using fresh duck breast and mushrooms. The same preparation may be used with quail.

Summer is the season for young ginger. The roots are bigger; the flavor milder. Older, winter roots are strong.

Leftover leg meat from ducks can be roasted and thinly sliced for salads. Skin can be crisped for cracklings and the carcass used for stock.

HU-NAN DUCK SAUCE

2 tablespoons soybean oil
¼ cup chopped onion
2 cloves garlic, crushed
¼ cup dry red wine
1½ cups CHINESE DUCK STOCK
  or Chicken Stock

1 teaspoon Cornstarch Slurry
1 tablespoon soy sauce
½ teaspoon cayenne pepper
  Salt to taste

1. Heat oil in wok. Stirfry onion and garlic until lightly browned. Add wine, soy sauce and cayenne.
2. Add CHINESE DUCK STOCK and Cornstarch Slurry. Reduce to one third to one half. Adjust seasoning and keep warm.

CHINESE DUCK STOCK

2 duck carcasses
2 medium carrots, cut up
1 large onion, cut up
2 ribs celery, cut up

1 tablespoon ginger peelings
1 teaspoon green peppercorns
2 star anise
4 quarts water

Combine all ingredients in a stock pot and bring to a boil. Simmer at least 2 hours, or until reduced by one half. Strain. Makes 2 quarts.

FRESH FRUIT

Seasonal fresh fruits (strawberries, kiwi, pineapple,
lychee, Asian pear, orange,
banana, peach, etc).

Raspberry Syrup

Clean and prepare at least 4 different types of fruit, cut as needed. On dessert plates, arrange fruit on or around pools of Raspberry Syrup.

Dinner for Four

Calamari Fritta

Brodetto con Pastina

Pesto Genovese

Osso Bucco Otello

Broccoli Agli Olio

Victor Salad

Cannoli

Wines:

With the Calamari—Le Sincette, 1985
With the Veal—Dolcetto "Cru Vignabajla," 1985

Lola DiStefano, Owner
Greg DiStefano and Claudia DiStefano Rudner, Managers
Jeffrey Gutstein, Chef

The Victor Cafe opened in 1918 as a gramaphone shop where music lovers could listen to new recordings over espresso and spumoni. Since those World War I days, the restaurant has been a haven for opera lovers. In 1933, Victor Cafe began to serve complete meals to the strains of Verdi and Puccini. Founded by the late John Di Stefano, the restaurant was named for the Victor Talking Machine Company in nearby Camden, New Jersey. The original "Nipper" dog statue still stands guard at a gramaphone high above the bar. The walls are covered with old records and photographs, many signed mementos of the young singing talents for whom Di Stefano was an unofficial "artist's" representative.

"We have one of the most extensive record collections in the country, including some very rare recordings," says Gregory DiStefano, grandson of the founder. "If our guests are not dining to Caruso, Chaliapin or Pavarotti, they may be entertained by one of our waiters, many of whom are aspiring singers."

One of those aspiring singers was a cocky neighborhood lad who coaxed extra food from the owners with a song. "Someday you'll pay to hear me sing!" Mario Lanza told them.

At Victor's you might be entertained by a contralto vocalizing at the next table or by an aspiring tenor from the Settlement Music School performing on the Restaurant's "stage."

The look of Victor's hasn't changed in a half century. But the food has. Chef Jeffrey Gutstein, the CIA-trained chef who has managed Victor's kitchen since 1981, revamped and refined the once primarily Southern Italian menu. The focus is now on the more sophisticated foods of Northern Italy, with some dishes renamed for opera characters.

"I am a creative chef, however, all my recipes are based upon traditional Italian dishes," says Gutstein.

1303 Dickinson Street

CALAMARI FRITTA

1 pound cleaned squid	Lemon juice
1 quart salad oil	Basil
Flour	Oregano
	Crushed red pepper

1. Gut and skin squid, remove beak (spine) and cut bodies into ¼″ rings. Rinse and pat dry; dust with flour.
2. Heat oil to 425° or just smoking. Fry squid for 45 seconds, stirring occasionally. Remove at once; drain.
3. Sprinkle lightly with lemon juice and pinches of basil, oregano and crushed red pepper. Serve immediately.

BRODETTO CON PASTINA

¼ pound fresh spinach	2 eggs, beaten
½ cup ditalini (¼″ tube) pasta	¼ pound pecorino or romano cheese, grated
1 quart CHICKEN STOCK	Salt and white pepper

1. Steam spinach; drain, cool, chop and set aside.
2. Cook pasta in boiling salted water until barely tender (al dente). Strain; rinse in cold water to stop cooking. Set aside.
3. Bring CHICKEN STOCK to a boil. Drizzle eggs into stock while whisking. Return to a boil and add reserved spinach, pasta, cheese, salt and pepper. Serve hot.

CHICKEN STOCK

2½ pounds chicken backs and
   necks
3 medium carrots, cut up
3 ribs celery, cut up
2 large onions, cut up

3 sprigs parsley
⅛ teaspoon thyme
1 bay leaf
2½ quarts (10 cups) cold water
   Salt and white pepper

1. Rinse bones. Place all ingredients except salt and white pepper in a stockpot. Bring to a boil. Cover and simmer 3 hours. Skim surface. Strain. Season. Chill or freeze until needed. Makes about 6 cups.

PESTO GENOVESE

1 ounce (1 bunch) fresh basil
   or ½ ounce (1 cup) dried
2 cloves garlic
1 cup olive oil
3 ounces (¾ cup) pine nuts

⅓ cup grated pecorino cheese
½ pound fresh thin spaghetti
   or spagattini
   Salt and pepper

1. In processor or blender, blend basil, garlic and ⅓ cup of oil. Add pinenuts and ⅓ cup more oil; process 30 seconds. Add cheese and remaining ⅓ cup oil; process 1 minute more, scraping down sides. Chill overnight.

2. Before serving, cook pasta in boiling salted water a few minutes until just tender, al dente. Drain. Serve with reserved pesto sauce brought to room temperature.

OSSO BUCCO OTELLO

8 ossibuchi, 1" to 1½" slices from veal shanks	6 ounces (¾ cup) frozen orange juice concentrate
Seasoned flour	2 tablespoons dry white wine
6 tablespoons salad oil	Zest of ½ orange rind
1 large onion, diced	Pinch of rosemary
2 cloves garlic	Salt and pepper
4 cups hot Chicken Stock	

1. Dredge shank pieces in flour. In large pan, with ¼ cup oil, fry shanks 1 minute on each side. Remove and set aside.
2. In same pan, add remaining 2 tablespoons oil and cook onion and garlic until limp. If pan will hold shanks in 1 layer, complete cooking on stove top. Otherwise, transfer shanks and onions to a large roasting pan to finish in oven.
3. To shanks and onions, add hot Chicken Stock, orange juice concentrate, white wine, orange zest and rosemary. If moved from fry pan, deglaze pan with wine and some stock. Add to roaster.
4. Cover pan tightly with lid or foil to retain steam.
5. Bring stock to a boil. Reduce to simmer, or place in 350-375° oven and cook 45 minutes. Shake pan occasionally to keep shanks from burning. Do not remove lid or foil for at least 45 minutes.
6. Vent steam carefully (away from you). Turn shanks and re-cover. Cook 40 minutes more or until fork tender.

BROCCOLI AGLI OLIO

1 bunch broccoli	2 tablespoons olive oil
1 clove garlic, minced	Salt and pepper

1. Trim broccoli base; separate or split into 4 stems. Blanch broccoli in boiling salted water for 2 minutes.
2. Meanwhile, heat oil in sauté pan and brown garlic. Add broccoli. Season with salt and pepper. Heat and serve.

VICTOR SALAD

1 head romaine lettuce
1 ripe tomato, cut in 8 wedges

VICTOR SALAD DRESSING
1 hardcooked egg, chopped

VICTOR SALAD DRESSING

½ cup salad oil
3 ounces gorgonzola cheese, crumbled
1 tablespoon red wine vinegar

½ teaspoon lemon juice
1 clove garlic, minced
Pinch of basil
Salt and pepper

1. Mix all ingredients together in container or blender. Cover and mix well. Makes 1 cup.

CANNOLI

½ pound sal-pak (dense) ricotta cheese
½ cup confectioners' sugar
½ cup heavy cream
½ teaspoon vanilla extract

⅓ cup semi-sweet chocolate minichips
4 *CANNOLI SHELLS*
Additional confectioners' sugar

In mixing bowl, combine ricotta and sugar. Stir in cream, vanilla and chocolate chips. Pipe or spoon into *CANNOLI SHELLS*. Sift confectioners' sugar over top.

The chef suggests adding 2 tablespoons chocolate liqueur with the chips or a nut-flavored liqueur if you make plain cheese cannoli, for extra flavor.

CANNOLI SHELLS

2 cups flour
2 tablespoons solid vegetable
   shortening
1 teaspoon sugar
¼ teaspoon salt

¾ cup Marsala wine
1 egg white, beaten
   Vegetable oil for deep frying

1. Have ready 4 metal tubes, 7" x 1 ⅛" in diameter, preferably of very light tin and not soldered.
2. In bowl, combine flour, shortening, sugar and salt. Add wine gradually, kneading to form a fairly stiff ball of dough. Cover with a towel and let stand 1 hour.
3. Cut dough in half; roll to ¼" or thinner. Cut into 4" squares. Place metal tube diagonally across square from point to point. Wrap dough around tube, overlapping other two points and seal with egg white.
4. Heat oil to 375°. Drop pastry-covered tubes, 1 or 2 at a time, into oil. Fry gently to golden brown. Remove. Let cool 2 minutes and gently slide shell from tube.
5. Repeat with remaining dough, reusing cooled tubes. Makes 10 to 12 cannoli shells.

Ready made cannoli shells are sold in some bakeries and markets. This recipe comes from Termini's, one of Philadelphia's foremost bakeries.

Dinner for Six

Grilled Shrimp and Pineapple

Wild Mushroom Enchiladas

Lemon Mousse with Brandy Snaps

Wines:

With the Shrimp—Sauvignon Blanc, Robert Pecota, 1985
With the Enchiladas—Zinfandel, Storybook Mountain,
1985

Judith Wicks, President
Wendy Born, General Manager
Kevin von Klause, Chef
Jerri Banks, Director of Wines

Our food is contemporary American, encompassing a broad range of regional cuisines and international influences," says Judy Wicks, who still lives over the cafe that she opened in 1983 as a coffee and muffin takeout shop.

The White Dog Cafe is now the prime dining attraction in its University City neighborhood, drawing students, stock brokers and suburbanites alike. It has spread into an adjacent brownstone and grown to seat 140.

With its neighbors La Terrasse, LeBus and the New Deck Tavern it is part of the bustling Sansom Street Restaurant Row in West Philadelphia.

Like the neighborhood, the foodstyle at the White Dog has developed steadily, growing from muffins to soups and sandwiches to wholesome, homey dinners and finally to a more sophisticted interpretation of American regional fare. From 1986, the Cafe's casual menu was given New American style at the hands of Aliza Green, formerly Executive Chef at both DiLullo's and Apropos. Chef Kevin von Klause succeeded her in the White Dog kitchen in September, 1987. Von Klause is a graduate of the Culinary Institute of America and worked with Green both here and at Apropos.

"Our direction is still geared towards locally produced ingredients and a seasonal menu," said von Klause. "Nothing too exotic, just a simple fare with a twist."

The wine list and beer selection at the White Dog also represent some of the best America has to offer. With it all, the Cafe is a happy blend of '80s Bohemia and the casual charm of exposed brick walls, blue and white checkered tablecloths, old oak tables, antique lamps and hanging fixtures. The sunny, window-walled back porch is a favorite brunch setting.

The White Dog is named for the canine credited with saving the life of the late Helena P. Blavatsky, a 19th century resident of the rowhouse and founder of the Theosophical Society. Displayed throughout the restaurant is a collection of knickknacks and pictures immortalizing both the Cafe's namesake and other personable pups.

3420 Sansom Street

GRILLED SHRIMP AND PINEAPPLE

30 *large shrimp (about*
1½ pounds, 21-25 count)
    LIME MARINADE
1 *small, ripe pineapple*
2 *large, ripe mangoes (soft,*
with no green on skin)

¼ *cup freshly squeezed lime*
juice (2 limes)
Honey, optional
1 *bunch (1 to 2 ounces) fresh*
basil, rolled and sliced thin

1. Peel shrimp, leaving the tail and the last ring of shell as a handle. (Freeze shells for use in fish or seafood stocks.) Devein shrimp.
2. Add shrimp to *LIME MARINADE*, stirring to coat. Let shrimp marinate at least 3 hours or overnight, refrigerated.
3. Shortly before serving, prepare grill, preferably using hardwood charcoal. Herb wood cuttings (such as thyme, sage or rosemary wood) add a special flavor when added at the last minute. A home-model electric grill or ridged grill/skillet may be used.
4. Split pineapple, pole to pole. Core and cut half of pineapple in 6 slices, ½" thick, center cut, leaving outer skin intact. (Use leftover pineapple for next day's salad.)
5. Holding mango flat, slice lengthwise, running knife flat along the pit. Cut or scrape flesh from pit. Scoop or scrape flesh from skin. Puree mango. If flesh is stringy or especially fibrous, strain through a sieve or food mill.
6. In bowl, whisk together mango puree and lime juice. Taste and, if desired, add 1 or 2 teaspoons honey. Set aside.
7. Grill shrimp and pineapple slices just until shrimp are opaque and pineapple slices are warmed and grill-marked.
8. Spoon mango purée, dividing evenly, onto 6 plates. Arrange 1 slice pineapple (to one side) and 5 shrimp (fanned opposite pineapple) on the purée. Garnish with basil.

LIME MARINADE

½ cup peanut oil
¼ cup freshly squeezed lime
    juice (2 limes)

2 shallots, finely chopped
   Kosher salt
   Freshly ground black pepper

In mixing bowl, whisk together oil, lime juice, shallots, and a pinch each of salt and pepper, to taste. Use to marinate shrimp or scallops. Makes ¾ cup.

WILD MUSHROOM ENCHILADAS

½ pound poblano peppers
1 pound tortillas, 12 large
   (10") or 24 small (6"),
   preferably white corn
¼ cup peanut oil
4 shallots, finely chopped
6 large cloves garlic
1 pound fresh wild or exotic
   mushrooms (shiitake,
   pleurotte, girolle, cepe,
   chanterelle, morel, etc.)*

1 pound white mushrooms,
   wiped clean, sliced
1½ pounds Chihuahua cheese,
   shredded
2 ounces (½ cup) shelled raw
   pumpkin seeds (pepitas)
½ pound ripe plum tomatoes,
   halved, seeded and diced
2 ounces fresh cilantro

1. In advance, roast peppers (see index). Peel; seed and cut in strips. Reserve. (Poblanos are dark green, mild and have a smokey taste. If unavailable, use green bell peppers and 2 jalapeno peppers.) Reserve.

2. Wrap tortillas in cloth and place in a colander over a pot of boiling water. Tortillas must be supple or they will split when rolled. Corn tortillas are especially prone to splitting.

3. In large skillet, heat oil and sauté shallots and garlic for 1 minute. Add reserved peppers, wild and white mushrooms. Cut large mushrooms; cook until limp.

4. Chop half of cilantro (2 tablespoons, tamped). Add to mushroom mixture. Stir in (1 pound) of cheese.

5. Divide and spoon filling evenly along center of each tortilla. Roll tortillas around filling and arrange, seam side down, in lightly oiled baking dish, 12" x 15" x 2" or larger. (Fit tortillas tightly.) Top with remaining cheese, tomato and pumpkin seeds.**

6. Meanwhile, preheat oven to 400°. Bake enchiladas for 15 to 20 minutes or until bubbling. Garnish with cilantro leaves. Makes 2 to 4 enchiladas per serving, depending on size of tortillas.

Dried mushrooms may be substituted in part.

To Reconstitute Dried Mushrooms: Cover mushrooms with warm water and let stand ½ hour or until softened. Remove and inspect for dirt. Strain liquid through clean cloth. Slice mushrooms if appropriate. Combine mushrooms and liquid in saucepan. Simmer until mushrooms have reabsorbed their essense. Use in recipe as directed.

***Recipe may be prepared ahead to this point and refrigerated for later use. Bake covered for 20 minutes at 400°; uncover and bake 10 minutes more.*

If white corn tortillas are not available, yellow corn or white flour tortillas may be substituted. Corn tortillas provide the best flavor; flour tortillas are easier to handle. Chihuahua cheese is a mild, creamy Muenster-like cheese made in a Mennonite community in Mexico's Chihuahua province. If unavailable, substitute Muenster or Monterey Jack. There is no substitute for the pungent flavor and aroma of cilantro.

LEMON MOUSSE WITH BRANDY SNAPS

10 *egg yolks*
 3 *cups sugar*
    Juice and zest of 2 large
    lemons

 6 *tablespoons unsalted butter,*
    at room temperature
1½ *cups heavy cream*
    Berries for garnish
    BRANDY SNAPS

1. In stainless steel bowl over simmering water, whisk egg yolks, sugar, lemon juice (at least ½ cup) and grated lemon rind until mixture thickens, about 10 minutes.

2. At the end, while custard is still warm, stir in softened butter. Cover closely with plastic wrap; chill.

3. Whip cream until soft peaks form. Folding gently, combine whipped cream and cool custard. Pour or spoon mousse into stemmed glasses (martini glasses are perfect) and chill. Serve with *BRANDY SNAPS.*

BRANDY SNAPS

½ cup unsalted butter	¼ teaspoon ground ginger
½ cup sugar	⅛ teaspoon ground cinnamon
⅓ cup dark molasses	10 tablespoons flour
1 teaspoon grated orange rind	2 tablespoons cognac

1. In stainless steel saucepan, combine butter, sugar, molasses, orange rind, ginger and cinnamon. Bring to a boil. Remove from heat. Let cool 5 minutes.

2. Gradually stir in flour and cognac. Keep batter warm over a hot water bath. Preheat oven to 350°.

3. On a parchment-lined or non-stick baking sheet, place a tablespoonful of batter and spread thin with back of spoon, forming a circle 4" to 5" in diameter. Allow ample space between cookies. Repeat with remaining batter. Depending on size of sheet, bake up to 6 cookies at a time. Bake at 350° until bubbling and browned, about 10 minutes.

4. While still warm, roll each cookie jellyroll-style around a ½" metal tube or dowel. Let cool. Store in airtight container. Makes about 20 cookies.

Brandy Snaps can be shaped over an inverted cup to form a serving cup.

DINING IN-WITH THE GREAT CHEFS
A collection of Gourmet Recipes from the finest chefs in the Country

☐ Dining In—Atlanta	$8.95	☐ Dining In—Monterey Peninsula	$7.95
☐ Dining In—Baltimore, Vol. II	8.95	☐ Dining In—Napa Valley	8.95
☐ Dining In—Boston	8.95	☐ Dining In—New Orleans	8.95
☐ Dining In—Chicago, Vol. III	8.95	☐ Dining In—Philadelphia, Vol. II	8.95
☐ Dining In—Cleveland	8.95	☐ Dining In—Phoenix	8.95
☐ Dining In—Dallas	8.95	☐ Dining In—Pittsburgh	7.95
☐ Dining In—Denver	7.95	☐ Dining In—Portland	7.95
☐ Dining In—Hampton Roads	8.95	☐ Dining In—St. Louis	7.95
☐ Dining In—Hawaii	8.95	☐ Dining In—Salt Lake City	8.95
☐ Dining In—Houston, Vol. II	8.95	☐ Dining In—San Francisco, Vol. II	8.95
☐ Dining In—Kansas City	8.95	☐ Dining In—Seattle	8.95
☐ Dining In—Los Angeles	8.95	☐ Dining In—Sun Valley	8.95
☐ Dining In—Manhattan	8.95	☐ Dining In—Toronto	7.95
☐ Dining In—Miami	8.95	☐ Dining In—Vancouver, B.C.	8.95
☐ Dining In—Milwaukee	8.95	☐ Dining In—Washington, D.C.	8.95
☐ Dining In—Minneapolis/St. Paul, Vol. II	8.95		

THE EPICURES
Menu Guides to the Better Restaurants in Each City

☐ Baltimore Epicure	$7.95	☐ Manhattan Epicure	$7.95
☐ Boston Epicure	7.95	☐ Miami Epicure	7.95
☐ Chicago Epicure	7.95	☐ Minneapolis/St. Paul Epicure	7.95
☐ Dallas Epicure	7.95	☐ New Orleans Epicure	7.95
☐ Denver Epicure	7.95	☐ San Diego Epicure	7.95
☐ Detroit Epicure	7.95	☐ San Francisco Epicure	7.95
☐ Honolulu Epicure	7.95	☐ Seattle Epicure	7.95
☐ Houston Epicure	7.95	☐ St. Louis Epicure	7.95
☐ Kansas City Epicure	7.95	☐ Washington D.C. Epicure	7.95
☐ Los Angeles Epicure	7.95	☐ The National Epicure	11.95

TO ORDER, SEND PRICE PLUS $1.00 POSTAGE AND HANDLING PER BOOK

☐ Check (✔) here if you woul like to have a different Dining In—Cookbook sent to you once a month. Payable by MasterCard or VISA. Returnable if not satisfied.

Simply fill out the order form or call... **1-800-426-5537**

BILL TO:

Name _____

Address_____

City _____ State___ Zip _____

SEND COMPLETED FORM TO:

PEANUT BUTTER PUBLISHING
329 2ND AVENUE WEST
SEATTLE, WA 98104
(206) 281-5965

DC DIW 3/87

SHIP TO:

Name _____

Address_____

City _____ State___ Zip _____

☐ **Payment Enclosed**   ☐ **Charge**

VISA # _____ Exp. _____

MasterCard # _____ Exp. _____

Signature_____